# The Question of Arbitrability

## Challenges to the Arbitrator's Jurisdiction and Authority

Mark M. Grossman

ILR Press
New York State School of
Industrial and Labor Relations
Cornell University

Cover design by Joe Gilmore
Composed by Eastern Graphics
Printed by Braun-Brumfield

ISBN 0-87546-106-9

Cataloguing in Publication Data
Grossman, Mark M., 1943-
    The question of arbitrability.
    Includes index.
    1. Grievance arbitration—United States. 2. Arbitra-
tors, Industrial—United States. 3. Jurisdiction—
United States. 4. Grievance procedures—United States.
I. Title.
KF3424.G76   1984        344.73'0189143        84-6568
ISBN 0-87546-106-9        347.304189143

Copies may be ordered from
ILR Press
New York State School of
Industrial and Labor Relations
Cornell University
Ithaca, NY 14853

Printed in the United States of America
54321

# Contents

# Introduction

ARBITRABILITY, the arbitrator's jurisdiction to hear a grievance on its merits, is an often misunderstood and misused term. There are many misconceptions of the scope of the arbitrator's authority to make rulings during the hearing, render decisions after the hearing, and impose remedies as part of the award. Despite all the court decisions dealing with them, these subjects still evoke uninformed and visceral reactions.

This book is intended to define for the labor relations practitioner the judicial role in determining the jurisdiction and authority of the arbitrator. It particularly emphasizes the distinction between the roles of the judge and the arbitrator in resolving issues of substantive arbitrability—as opposed to procedural arbitrability, the question of whether contract grievance procedures were complied with, which is an issue for the arbitrator to resolve—and the scope of the arbitrator's authority. Although union and management may agree to submit questions of the arbitrator's jurisdiction and authority directly to the arbitrator, they should have a clear understanding of whether these questions will be decided by the courts if they are submitted to that forum.

The labor relations practitioner must be aware of the various types of challenges to the arbitrator's jurisdiction and authority; the applicability of a presumption favoring arbitrability; the extent to which the court will defer to the arbitrator's findings and judgments; and the differences between the public and private sectors.

It is in the interests of all parties to understand the "rules" of arbitration from the outset. It is to the union's advantage to be aware of when it has a right to resolve a dispute through arbitration and when it does not. A long grievance and arbitration procedure in which the final award is blocked before its issuance or vacated afterward consumes time and money that could have been more effectively used to find another means of resolving the primary dispute. It is not in management's interest to refuse frivolously to proceed in arbitration or implement an arbitration award. Good will developed over a long relationship can be dissipated by the ignorance of one party that is perceived by the other side as bad faith.

This book explores the important judicial decisions on questions of arbitrability and the arbitrator's authority, including the following:

In the absence of its agreement to arbitrate, may a party be compelled to submit a dispute to arbitration?

Does the court interpret the arbitration agreement in order to determine arbitrability?

Under what circumstances does the arbitrator determine arbitrability?

Is the fact that a topic is a permissive bargaining subject relevant in determining arbitrability?

What is the relevancy of the requested remedy in determining arbitrability?

Does a judicial determination of arbitrability affect the determination of the merits of the grievance?

How does the expiration of the collective bargaining agreement affect a grievance?

Is the potential magnitude of labor unrest considered in determining arbitrability?

Will the court order tripartite arbitration covering three parties of interest in absence of an agreement by the parties to submit to such a process?

If the parties to an arbitration cannot agree on the issue to be submitted, may the party who alleges to be aggrieved proceed?

What effect has the language "the arbitrator shall not have the power to add to, subtract from, or modify the collective bargaining agreement"?

Does a stipulated issue affect the arbitrator's authority?

Can the arbitrator possess greater authority than that of the parties?

Is an arbitrator required to explain the rationale for the award?

Does an arbitrator have authority to award punitive damages?

Is an error of law or fact a proper basis for vacating an arbitration award?

After the issuance of an arbitration award, may a court on its own motion raise a question of the unenforceability of a contract provision?

Although the first seven chapters deal with private sector law, these discussions are also applicable in many respects to the public sector. Chapters 8 through 11 are devoted to explaining the unique aspects of the public sector.

# 1.

## Basic Considerations

### In Which Forum Are the Issues Resolved?

THE PARTIES may agree to submit questions related to jurisdiction or scope of the arbitrator's authority directly to the arbitrator. Absent any such agreement, the court is the proper forum for determining the jurisdiction and scope of authority. This discussion assumes that the parties have not agreed to submit these issues to the arbitrator, unless otherwise indicated.

### Who Raises the Issues?

The party seeking to avoid arbitration or limit the scope of the arbitration raises the issue of the arbitrator's jurisdiction or authority. Although usually the union is the party seeking arbitration and management is the party raising the question of arbitrability, the positions of the parties are occasionally reversed, for example, when the employer requests a strike injunction. The employer asserts that the dispute is covered by the arbitration agreement. The union, in its defense, may assert that the dispute is not covered by the arbitration agreement and is, therefore, not arbitrable. In such a situation the court resolves the arbitrability issue in order to determine whether or not to grant the injunction. It will enjoin a strike if the strike is over a dispute the parties have agreed to resolve by arbitration.[1]

## When Do the Issues Arise?

### Before Submitting a Dispute to Arbitration

A party seeking to arbitrate a grievance pursuant to an agreement to arbitrate may seek a court order to compel arbitration. If the opposing side does not believe the matter arbitrable, it can raise arbitrability as a defense.

If the collective bargaining agreement permits an ex parte initiation of the arbitration process, the party objecting to arbitration may challenge arbitrability in a court action to enjoin the proceeding.

### During the Arbitration Hearing

The parties may submit an arbitrability challenge directly to the arbitrator. A waiver of the right to raise the issue in court may result from either submission of the issue to the arbitrator or proceeding on the merits without reserving the right to subsequently challenge arbitrability.

### After the Arbitration Award

The jurisdiction of the arbitrator to hear the case may be challenged after the issuance of an arbitration award only if such right was not waived by participating in the arbitration or by delegating the resolution of the arbitrability issue to the arbitrator. In addition, challenges to the arbitrator's

---

1. Boys Market, Inc. v. Retail Clerks Union Local 770, 398 U.S. 235, 74 L.R.R.M. 2257 (1970).

ruling, decision, and remedy may be brought to court after the issuance of an arbitration award.

Generally, these arbitrability challenges are raised by a motion in court to vacate the award. They may also be raised as a defense to a motion to confirm the award. Neither the arbitrator nor the prevailing party has the authority to enforce the arbitration award. But, once the award is confirmed by a court, it may be enforced in a similar manner to the enforcement of any other court order.

The statute of limitation, which specifies the amount of time permitted to bring a motion for vacating an award, may be shorter than that for a motion to confirm. If so, the defense of nonarbitrability may be found to be untimely if it is raised after it could have been raised in a motion to vacate.

## Steelworkers Trilogy

Three 1960 Supreme Court decisions known as the Steelworkers Trilogy guide today's judicial determinations of arbitrability.[2]

The Court noted that the parties cannot foresee every contingency, and therefore, their contract must be interpreted in light of the common law of the shop.

> The collective bargaining agreement states the rights and duties of the parties. It is more than a contract; it is a generalized code to govern a myriad of cases, which the draftsmen cannot wholly anticipate.[3]

---

2. United Steelworkers of America v. American Manufacturing Co., 363 U.S. 564, 46 L.R.R.M. 2423 (1960); United Steelworkers of America v. Warrior & Gulf Navigation Co., 363 U.S. 574, 46 L.R.R.M. 2416 (1960); United Steelworkers of America v. Enterprise Wheel and Car Corp., 363 U.S. 593, 46 L.R.R.M. 2423 (1960).

3. Warrior & Gulf, *supra* note 1, at 578.

The Court observed that arbitrators are selected on the basis of their knowledge of the industry and that

> [t]he ablest judge could not be expected to bring the same experience and competence to bear upon the determination of a grievance, because he cannot be similarly informed.[4]

The Court stated that, as a matter of federal policy and pursuant to section 203(d) of the Labor-Management Relations Act, grievance arbitration is the desirable method for resolving labor disputes. It explained that if full effect were not accorded the arbitration process, the result would be a crippling effect on that process. It viewed the arbitration clause as the quid pro quo for the no-strike clause and the arbitration process as having therapeutic value and being a stabilizing influence.

While no party can be compelled to submit to arbitration a matter that was not agreed to, the burden of proof for a party arguing nonarbitrability is extremely great.

> An order to arbitrate a particular grievance should not be denied unless it may be said with *positive assurance* that the arbitration clause is not susceptible to an interpretation that covers the asserted dispute. Doubts should be resolved in favor of coverage. (emphasis added)[5]

The Trilogy cases dealt with two questions of the scope of the arbitrator's authority: whether the dispute sought to be arbitrated fell within the ambit of the arbitration clause and whether the arbitrator's remedy was proper. The decisions in these cases established a presumption in favor of the arbitrator's jurisdiction and authority in the context of the issues then before the Court. That presumption does not necessarily apply in other issues of the arbitrator's jurisdiction and authority.

---

4. *Id.* at 582.

5. *Id.*

# 2.

## Proper Parties

### Employers

THE ISSUE of whether an employer must submit to arbitration frequently arises in the cases of successor employers and multiemployer associations. In these situations, the employer maintains that, although a labor contract containing an arbitration clause may exist, it is not a party to that contract, and therefore, the contract may not be enforced against it.

### Successor Employers
There are three significant Supreme Court decisions concerning successor employers. In the first, *Wiley and Sons* v. *Livingston*, decided in 1964, the Court held that

> the disappearance by merger of a corporate employer which has entered into a collective bargaining agreement with a union does not automatically terminate all rights of the employees covered by the agreement, and that, in appropriate circumstances, present here, the successor employer may be required to arbitrate with the union under the agreement.[1]

The decision in *Wiley* was primarily based on the fact that the union had no say in the corporate change, which was

---

1. 376 U.S. 543, 548, 55 L.R.R.M. 2769, 2772 (1964).

unilaterally instituted by the employer, and the national labor policy favoring arbitration. In addition, the Court stated unequivocally that the issues of whether the contract still existed after the merger, whether the new employer was bound to arbitrate, and what questions were to be arbitrated were for the courts to resolve.

While the substantive decision in *Wiley* was circumscribed by the Court's subsequent decisions in *NLRB* v. *Burns International Security Services, Inc.*[2] and *Howard Johnson Company* v. *Detroit Joint Board,*[3] the determination that the courts and not the arbitrator are to resolve whether the new employer is bound to arbitrate remains unaltered.

The Court distinguished *Burns* from *Wiley* on the basis that *Wiley* involved a merger in a state where the law required the surviving corporation to be liable for the obligations of the disappearing corporation. In *Burns,* the new employer was selected by competitive bidding and had no dealings with the prior employer. The Court found that there was no continuity of business interest between Burns and its predecessor and that Burns could not be bound to proceed in arbitration under the prior employer's contract. This was held despite the fact that Burns hired substantially the same work force to perform the same duties as the prior employer. Any other decision, the Court noted, would stifle the free transfer of capital. The Court concluded that the new employer must have the unfettered right to make changes in the operation of the enterprise.

In the *Howard Johnson* case, one employer bought the property of another, but the Court held that no obligation to arbitrate existed under the prior employer's contract because a substantial percentage of employees was not re-

---

2. 406 U.S. 272, 80 L.R.R.M. 2225 (1972).

3. 417 U.S. 249, 86 L.R.R.M. 2449 (1974).

tained, and there was no agreement for the new employer to assume the liabilities of the prior employer.

Summing up the Court decisions, the national labor policy favoring arbitration must be weighed against inhibition of the free transfer of capital. The criteria to be applied are the connection between subsequent and prior employers; continuity of business operations; continuity of work force; and whether the new employer is to be liable for obligations of the prior employer. Apparently, the new employer will not be held to the labor contract unless the facts substantially satisfy these criteria.

Of course, if other factors exist, these could become determinative, for example, the union's abandonment of the contract or the change in ownership prompted by other than legitimate business reasons.

While the question of whether the subsequent employer is required to arbitrate is for the court, in *Steelworkers* v. *U.S. Gypsum Co.* a court of appeals has held that it is for the arbitrator to determine which provisions of the contract, if any, are binding on the successor employer. This should not be confused with the Supreme Court's decision in *Wiley* that the court is to determine which questions may be presented to the arbitrator. Holding the grievance arbitrable is not "even a remote suggestion of how the merits are to, or must, be determined" and does not "begin to put an advance court imprimatur on the award."[4]

The court makes an interesting observation in footnote 11. Once the employer is bound to arbitrate under the contract, it is not necessarily bound to the provisions of the contract. The court is not determining that the provisions are binding as a condition precedent to arbitration. It is merely determining that the arbitrator has the power to find the provisions binding.

---

4. 492 F.2d 713, 718, 85 L.R.R.M. 2962, 2965 (5th Cir. 1974).

The appeals court caveat probably does not have wide application. In the more routine cases, there is no doubt that the provision will be found binding. Once the court determines the arbitration provision is binding, it is quite likely that the arbitrator will find other provisions to be binding. But there may be some anomalous provisions that may be held to be not applicable in the new environment, and the court apparently has provided flexibility for such provisions.

### Multiemployer Associations

In situations where a group of employers acting through an association bargains with one union, despite the facts that the bargaining units are certified individually and no party is compelled to agree to multiemployer bargaining, the arbitrability issue arises when the union seeks to enforce the multiemployer contract against an employer who claims it is not bound to the contract. This question is appropriate for the court to resolve.

An employer may withdraw from a multiemployer association before the commencement of collective bargaining by communicating an unambiguous intent to withdraw. An attempt to withdraw after the commencement of negotiations, however, has been held to be untimely.[5] The Supreme Court has recently ruled that the existence of an impasse in bargaining does not provide a basis for an employer to withdraw from a multiemployer association.[6]

## Unions

Not only do the courts determine whether an employer is bound to arbitrate, they also determine whether the em-

---

5. Carvel Co. v. NLRB, 560 F.2d 1030, 96 L.R.R.M. 2107 (1st Cir. 1977).

6. Charles D. Bonanno Linen Service, Inc. v. NLRB, 455 U.S. 404, 109 L.R.R.M. 2257 (1982).

ployer may invoke arbitration. Just as an employer may not be compelled to arbitrate unless it is bound by an agreement to arbitrate, a union will not be required to arbitrate absent its agreement to arbitrate. In *Atkinson* v. *Sinclair Refining Co.* the Supreme Court held that, where the grievance procedure permits only the union to file grievances, the employer may not compel arbitration of a claim for damages for the breach of the no-strike provision of the contract.[7] Thus, the fact that the collective bargaining agreement contains an arbitration provision does not mean that the union may be the respondent in an arbitration. That can only happen if the contract authorizes the employer to initiate grievances.

Just as an employer may not compel arbitration if the contract extends the right to initiate grievances only to the union, individual employees may not initiate grievances in such cases, even though that union represents the employees and bargains on their behalf.[8]

An interesting question that will probably lead to more litigation is whether an employee may participate in an arbitration that will affect his or her rights, while the union is representing an employee with a conflicting position. A typical example is a promotion case in which the union is representing the most senior employee, who did not receive a promotion, and the employee who was promoted seeks to intervene in the case. Only recently have any

---

7. 370 U.S. 238, 50 L.R.R.M. 2433 (1962).

8. Hines and Carroll v. Brotherhood of RR Trainmen, 417 F.2d 1025, 72 L.R.R.M. 2614 (1st Cir. 1969). If an employee believes his or her union did not properly represent him or her, the employee does have the right to sue the union for a breach of the duty of fair representation and the right to commence a section 301 contract suit against the employer. Such a suit against the employer does not vacate or modify an arbitration award and is separate from any arbitration award obtained by the union. Before proceeding against the employer, the employee will be required to establish that the union did not properly represent him or her in the grievance procedure.

questions been raised about whether the employee who was not promoted has the right to participate. In any event, it may be within the arbitrator's discretionary powers to permit the employee to participate.

## Successor Unions

Changes of the certified representative of the employees occur from time to time. The newly certified union automatically succeeds to the rights of its predecessor and may initiate grievances arising under an existing contract. The newly certified union may also opt to repudiate the contract and immediately commence bargaining for a new contract. The previously certified union will be permitted to continue to represent the employees in an arbitration case where there is no strong indication that such action will lead to labor unrest.[9] This is reasonable because the newly certified union might be disadvantaged by not having participated in the negotiations and not having its own stewards in the field at the time the grievance occurred. In *Steelworkers* v. *U.S. Gypsum Co.* the court, commenting on an employer's claim that a decertified union could no longer process a grievance, found no conflict between the limited postdecertification recognition and the policies sought to be achieved by the federal labor law.[10]

## Joint Bargaining

Interesting variations of the union's right to arbitrate can occur when a union engages in joint collective bargaining. If a certified union bargains jointly with another certified union and executes with an employer a single contract cov-

---

9. ILWU Local 142 v. Land and Construction Co., 498 F.2d 201, 86 L.R.R.M. 2874 (9th Cir. 1974). The court expressed no opinion concerning the disposition of the case if the newly certified union had sought to be a party.

10. U.S. Gypsum, *supra* note 4.

ering both units, each union is entitled to raise and process its own grievances to arbitration. If two unions are jointly certified, either union by itself may initiate arbitration if the other union's participation or authorization is considered merely proper, as opposed to necessary.

## Interunion Conflict

The courts' pragmatic approach to resolving arbitrability challenges, demonstrated by the practice of assessing the magnitude of labor unrest in determining whether a decertified union may continue to process a grievance, is also evident in decisions concerning interunion and potential interunion disputes. In these cases, the right of a union to participate in an arbitration is significantly affected by whether or not a competing union's rights are involved. In *Machinists* v. *Howmet Corp. Inc.,* the court rejected a union's request for arbitration because it would not avoid industrial strife.[11] The union representing employees of a closed plant sought to arbitrate what rights these employees would have at another of the employer's plants, where the employees were represented by another union.

In another case, the court ordered two unions and an employer involved in a jurisdictional dispute to tripartite arbitration. The union that lost the arbitration sought to vacate the award on the grounds that the arbitrator exceeded his authority by considering the National Labor Relations Board (NLRB) certification and not limiting his examination to the scope of the collective bargaining agreement between the employer and that union.[12] The union's claim

---

11. 466 F.2d 1249, 81 L.R.R.M. 2289 (9th Cir. 1972).

12. Textron, Inc. v. Auto Workers, Local 516, 500 F.2d 921, 86 L.R.R.M. 3240 (2d Cir. 1974).

questioned the authority to expand the bilateral arbitration agreement to involve another party. The court held that developing common law of labor contracts permitted the compulsion of tripartite arbitration and that the arbitrator could rely on any relevant evidence.

# 3.

# The Agreement to Arbitrate

AFTER ASCERTAINING the proper parties, the next considerations in determining arbitrability are whether the contract contains an arbitration clause; whether the contract had actually become effective; whether the contract has expired; and whether a particular contract benefit may have vested during the contract term even though the benefit may not be realized until after the expiration of the contract.

## Is There an Arbitration Clause?

If the collective bargaining agreement provides for a method of dispute resolution other than arbitration, the courts will not compel arbitration. In *Printing Pressmen, No. 57* v. *Florida Publishing Co.*, the contract provided that unresolved disputes be brought before a joint board consisting of an equal number of management and labor representatives. Because this procedure did not provide for a neutral party to make a binding decision and was likely to result in a deadlock over controversial issues, the court ruled there was no agreement to arbitrate.[1]

---

1. 468 F.2d 824, 81 L.R.R.M. 2561 (5th Cir. 1972).

The determination of whether or not a party is committed to arbitration is for the courts to decide.[2] Despite the national policy favoring arbitration as a means to resolve contract disputes, the courts will not compel a reluctant party to submit a dispute to arbitration,

> unless under a fair construction of the agreement he is bound to do so. Absent a contractual obligation to the contrary, a reluctant party is free to pursue any available legal remedy to redress its grievances.[3]

Although arbitration is a preferred method for resolving disputes, it is not required. In *Oil, Chemical & Atomic Workers, Local 8-831* v. *Mobil Oil Corp.* the court stated that the sine qua non for requiring arbitration is a contract between the parties binding them to this extrajudicial method of resolving disputes.[4] In this case the parties had a grievance and arbitration clause in the contract; however, the contract also provided that nothing would prevent either party from applying to court for relief. The court rules that this option negated the mandatory aspect of the contractual grievance procedure, and it declined to compel arbitration.

## Is the Contract in Effect?

When an agreement did not take effect because the notice of ratification was not given to the employer as required in the contract and other evidence established that no contract ex-

---

2. Atkinson v. Sinclair Refining Co., 370 U.S. 238, 50 L.R.R.M. 2433 (1962).

3. Boeing Co. v. UAW, 370 F.2d 969, 970, 64 L.R.R.M. 2208 (3d Cir. 1969).

4. 441 F.2d 651, 77 L.R.R.M. 2062 (3d Cir. 1971).

isted, an arbitration award concerning the discharge of strikers was vacated.[5]

## Has the Contract Expired?

It is an accepted principle of labor relations that the expiration of a contract does not vitiate or nullify a grievance that arose during the term of the contract. This is true even when the grievance is not filed until after the contract has expired. The commencement of the arbitration hearing and the date of the arbitration award are likewise not determinative of whether a grievance is arbitrable. Furthermore, the collective bargaining agreement is not terminated merely by the employer going out of business.[6]

If the objection to arbitration is based on the argument that the contract terminated and there is no allegation that the benefit was intended to continue beyond the contract expiration, the court will resolve the issue of whether the contract terminated as a matter of contract law. In one situation, the parties agreed that promotion language would survive the current contract but would terminate when the employee retired, resigned, or was discharged for cause. The district court held that the contract expired if the employee was discharged for cause and that the court should determine if there was cause.[7]

Another case that required the court to determine whether a contract existed was *Electrical Workers, IBEW, Local 278* v. *Jetero Corp.*[8] The employer had agreed to be

5. Globe Seaways, Inc. v. National Marine Engineers' Beneficial Ass'n, 451 F.2d 1159, 79 L.R.R.M. 2067 (2d Cir. 1971).

6. Bressette v. International Talc Co., 527 F.2d 211, 91 L.R.R.M. 2077 (2d Cir. 1975).

7. TWA v. Beaty, 402 F. Supp. 652, 91 L.R.R.M. 2087 (S.D.N.Y. 1975).

8. 496 F.2d 661, 88 L.R.R.M. 2184 (5th Cir. 1974), *aff'g* 88 L.R.R.M. 2185 (DC TEX 1973).

bound by the 1970 contract and amendments between the union and its association. The union claimed that the 1972 contract constituted the amendments referred to in the 1970 contract. The court of appeals sustained the district court decision holding that the employer was not bound to the 1972 contract and vacating the arbitration award. The district court noted that while the court generally is not to substitute its interpretation of the contract for the arbitrator's, it must resolve the issue of whether the employer is bound to the contract.

> A certain amount of contract interpretation is inherently involved in determining whether the parties give the arbitrator the power to make an award. Such contractual interpretation is not prohibited by the Steelworkers Trilogy.[9]

In another case, *Local 92* v. *News Free Press Co.*, the issue was remanded to the district court for a determination of whether a contract that contained an interest arbitration clause remained in force after the written expiration date and while the parties were negotiating a successor agreement.[10]

There is no question but that the courts are to resolve the issue of whether a party is bound to arbitrate. When that issue arises as a defense to an order to compel arbitration, the court will make a decision and may have to interpret the contract to some extent. In the *Electrical Workers* case, the court was asked to vacate an arbitration award. Despite the fact that an arbitrator concluded that the 1972 contract constituted amendments to the 1970 contract, the court did not defer to the arbitrator's award even though a contract interpretation was necessary to determine whether a party was bound to arbitrate.[11] Thus the court determina-

---

9. *Id.* at 2188.

10. 524 F.2d 1305, 90 L.R.R.M. 3000 (6th Cir. 1975).

11. Electrical Workers, *supra* note 8.

tion will be the same whether the issue is raised before or after an arbitration. The arbitrator's award will have little, if any, bearing on the court's decision.

Yet if the parties by their own terminology specifically limit all claims to ones arising during the contract, any claim that is alleged to have arisen after the contract termination will be dismissed by the courts. In *General Warehousemen & Employees Union Local 636 v. J. C. Penney Co.* the contract provided for arbitration of "a dispute or claim arising under and during the term" of the contract. The district court held the matter not arbitrable.[12]

## Are There Vested Rights?

Some aspects of the agreement may extend even beyond the expiration date of the contract. Rights may be accrued during the term of a contract and may not be intended to be realized until after the expiration date of the contract.[13] The claim that a particular provision of the contract was intended to survive the expiration date of the contract is a matter to be resolved by the arbitrator.[14] It is treated as a routine contract interpretation question. So long as it is claimed that the alleged rights arise from a contract containing an arbitration clause, the arbitrator will be permitted to determine the nature and extent of the agreement, even though the act that created the cause of action did not occur until after the contract expiration date.

---

12. 484 F. Supp. 130, 103 L.R.R.M. 2618 (DC PA 1980).

13. John Wiley and Sons v. Livingston, 376 U.S. 543, 55 L.R.R.M. 2769 (1964).

14. Nolde Bros. v. Bakery Workers, 430 U.S. 243, 94 L.R.R.M. 2753 (1977).

# 4.

# The Scope of
# the Arbitration Agreement

ONCE IT HAS been determined that the proper parties are involved and that they have agreed to arbitrate disputes, the courts should resolve the question of whether the particular dispute sought to be arbitrated falls within the province of the arbitration clause.

> Arbitration is a matter of contract and a party cannot be required to submit to arbitration any dispute which he has not agreed to submit.[1]

The federal policy favoring arbitration of labor disputes applies to the question of whether a dispute comes within the ambit of the arbitration clause. The court will review the grievance to determine if a colorable claim on the merits has been presented. It determines only whether or not the charging party's allegation comes under the arbitration clause.[2] Where a dispute as to whether a contract provision covers a specific situation requires the interpretation

---

1. Atkinson v. Sinclair Refining Co., 370 U.S. 238, 241, 50 L.R.R.M. 2433, 2435 (1962).

2. Bricklayers, Local 6 v. Boyd G. Heminger, Inc., 483 F.2d 129, 84 L.R.R.M. 2033 (6th Cir. 1973).

or application of the contract provision, the court will find the matter arbitrable unless it can be shown with positive assurance that the matter is not arbitrable.[3]

The paramount factor in determining whether a claim falls within the ambit of the arbitration clause is the scope of that clause. The nature and extent of the article in the contract governing arbitration is usually determined by the section defining a grievance. If one were to ask a labor relations student, "What is the definition of a grievance?," the answer would probably be "a complaint of any employee" or "a complaint of an employee concerning some aspect of his employment." This definition may be appropriate for an NLRB analysis of a charge that an employee's discharge was precipitated by his or her filing a grievance. In a discussion of arbitrability, however, the correct answer to that question is "whatever the parties define a grievance to be in their contract."

The remedy requested by the aggrieved party is usually viewed as a suggestion to the arbitrator and not as the basis for determining the arbitrability of the particular grievance. There are three types of definitions of the term *grievance*: a definition in broad terms (any dispute); a definition limited to questions of contract interpretation or application; and a definition containing exclusionary language.

## Broad Grievance Definition

The broadest possible language specifies that "any dispute" may be raised in the arbitration procedure. The party seeking arbitration is not required to allege a violation of the collective bargaining agreement. The grievant has only to

---

3. United Steelworkers of America v. Warrior & Gulf Navigation Co., 363 U.S. 574, 46 L.R.R.M. 2416 (1960); IAM v. Fraser & Johnston Co., 454 F.2d 88, 79 L.R.R.M. 2118 (9th Cir. 1971).

raise a claim tangentially affecting the employment relationship.

Basing its decision on a broad grievance definition in the contract, the Supreme Court held arbitrable a claim by mine workers that the mine operators' continued employment of a foreman who habitaully did not adhere to prescribed mine safety procedures constituted a safety hazard.[4] A similar claim under a narrower definition of grievance was held not arbitrable by a court of appeals.[5]

In another case, the union's claim that a sham corporation was established in order to circumvent the union security agreement was held arbitrable on the basis of a broad definition of grievance.[6] The dissenting opinion would have held the matter not arbitrable because it raised the issue of whether one company could be bound to the agreement of another employer.

Another illustration of the scope of a broad arbitration clause is found in a case where a union claimed that the oral agreement to end a strike also contained a wage increase. The court held the matter arbitrable, even though the alleged agreement was made after the contract under which the matter was arbitrated.[7]

Judging from these examples, if the grievance definition is broad, the court will permit an extremely wide spectrum of issues to be presented to the arbitrator.

There are some situations where defining a grievance as

---

4. Gateway Coal Co. v. United Mine Workers of America, 414 U.S. 368, 85 L.R.R.M. 2049 (1974).

5. United Steelworkers of America, Local No. 1617 v. General Fireproofing Co., 464 F.2d 726, 80 L.R.R.M. 3113 (6th Cir. 1972).

6. Bricklayers, *supra* note 2.

7. United Engineering & Foundry Employees Ass'n Independent Union v. United Engineering & Foundry Co., 389 F.2d 479, 67 L.R.R.M. 2168 (3d Cir. 1967).

"any dispute" may lead to ambiguities. While it creates a right to arbitrate, does it also establish the substantive right sought to be arbitrated? For example, what if under a contract that contains no substantive contract clause covering review of disciplinary actions, an employee is fired? If a grievance is "any dispute," the union clearly has a right to grieve the discharge, and there is no necessity to establish a violation of an explicit provision of the contract. Is the arbitrator to impose a just cause standard? Or, what if a union claims the employees' work load exceeds a fair day's work? Is the arbitrator to apply the standard enunciated in the union grievance? Is he or she to apply a standard that the work load must not be unduly burdensome?

## Limited Grievance Definition

The most common grievance language limits the arbitrator to hearing an issue of an interpretation or application of the collective bargaining agreement. The court will not attempt to prejudge a union claim of contract violation by examining whether the language could reasonably be interpreted in a manner that would sustain the union's claim. The contract language may not even mention the subject matter sought to be arbitrated.

> Explicit language in collective bargaining agreements covering each specific claim alleged to be arbitrated is not required. We have held that the complete silence of an agreement on the issue sought to be arbitrated is not sufficient evidence to meet the rigorous standard set by the Steelworker Trilogy for a finding of nonarbitrability.[8]

The courts recognize that the parties may not have expressly contemplated the situation leading to the grievance but may

---

8. Machinists v. Howmet Corp., 466 F.2d 1249, 1252, 81 L.R.R.M. 2289, 2291 (9th Cir. 1972).

have covered it in their broader conceptual agreement.[9] It is impractical, if not impossible, for the parties to create a contract to cover specifically every contingency.

Nevertheless, despite a party's allegation that a particular contract clause has been violated, the courts will, with appropriate proof, hold a matter nonarbitrable. In a case in which the contract did not contain a layoff provision, a side letter established that that topic was to be left for future negotiations. Further negotiations were conducted without an agreement on layoffs, and the court held there was no right to arbitrate.[10]

The definition of grievance may also be tightened to preclude implied meanings of the contract. In *IEU* v. *General Electric Co.* the court dealt with contract language that limited a grievance to an allegation of "direct violation of the express purpose of the contractual provision in question."[11] It held nonarbitrable, therefore, a claim that the employer could not require a reasonable amount of overtime work because the contract contained an implied limitation on involuntary overtime.

While grievance language that covers any and all disputes is broad and all-inclusive, a clause that provides for "any and all disputes *hereunder*" was held to limit grievances to disputes under the contract.[12]

Occasionally, the grievance definition specifies a substantive right in addition to the general right to arbitrate

9. Association of Industrial Scientists v. Shell Development Co., 348 F.2d 385, 59 L.R.R.M. 2770 (9th Cir. 1965).

10. Radio Corp. v. Association of Scientists & Professional Engineering Personnel, 414 F.2d 893, 71 L.R.R.M. 3196 (3d Cir. 1969).

11. 450 F.2d 1295, 78 L.R.R.M. 2867 (2d Cir. 1971).

12. Rochdalle Village, Inc. v. Local 80, 605 F.2d 1290, 102 L.R.R.M. 2476 (2d Cir. 1979).

contract disputes. For instance, a grievance may be defined as both a dispute over an interpretation of the contract and a specific claim, such as that an employee was discharged without just cause. The grievance definition might also include the violation of past practice. Does the arbitrator or the court determine the nature and extent of the substantive right? Would the court resolve a dispute over the right because it is provided for in the grievance section and thereby relates to the arbitrator's authority? Or would the arbitrator determine the meaning because it constitutes a contract interpretation?

It is more logical for the arbitrator to determine the meaning of the clause. The substantive right could have been just as easily expressed in another provision of the contract. There is no special significance in the fact that the right was stated in the grievance provision. The arbitrator will have to interpret the grievance language in this situation just as he or she does when questions of procedural arbitrability arise.

## Exclusionary Grievance Definition

The third type of arbitration clause is one in which matters are specifically excluded from the definition of grievance. If the parties' own language clearly and unequivocally states that a matter is outside the scope of the grievance procedure, the court will not order a party to arbitrate that matter.

Even in these cases, however, the Supreme Court, applying the federal policy favoring arbitration, has determined that the party arguing nonarbitrability bears an extremely high burden of proof.

In the absence of any express provision excluding a particular grievance from arbitration, we think only the most forceful evidence of a purpose to exclude the claim from arbitration can prevail, particularly where, as here, the exclusionary clause is vague and the arbitration clause quite broad.[13]

Although the general rule is that the question of whether the contract terminated is for the court to resolve, in *Local 14, IBEW* v. *Radio Thirteen Eighty, Inc.* the court ruled that it was a question for the arbitrator.[14] The ruling was based upon the fact that the contract contained broad arbitration language and vague exclusionary language.

The exclusionary language will be applied despite the fact that a managerial action not subject to arbitration affects a matter covered by another provision of the agreement that does fall under the arbitration procedure. In a relevant case, a contract clause contained strong management rights language that included the right to control, operate, and assign work. These matters were designated as not covered by the arbitration clause. The court held the claim not arbitrable even though the managerial acts sought to be reviewed affected seniority, resulted in the reassignment of work outside the bargaining unit, and generated layoffs.[15]

If a dispute is apparently covered by both a contract provision that is not subject to arbitration and one that is subject to arbitration, the court will determine which clause governs on the basis of which is more specific. In one case, the contract excluded matters concerning the status of an employee under an employee benefit plan, which included retirement.[16] An employee who was forced to take disabil-

---

13. Warrior & Gulf, *supra* note 3. *See also* Machinists, *supra* note 8; Carpenters Council v. Brady Corp., 513 F.2d 1, 88 L.R.R.M. 3281 (10th Cir. 1975).

14. 469 F.2d 610, 81 L.R.R.M. 2829 (8th Cir. 1972).

15. Engineers v. General Electric Co., 531 F.2d 1178, 91 L.R.R.M. 2471 (3d Cir. 1976).

16. Local 2-124 v. American Oil Co., 528 F.2d 252, 91 L.R.R.M. 2202 (10th Cir. 1976).

ity retirement sought arbitration under the just cause provision of the collective bargaining agreement. The court ruled that even though the result of involuntary retirement was the same as discharge, some effect had to be given to the language that excluded from arbitration disputes under the employee benefit plan provision. It therefore found the dispute nonarbitrable.

In a similar finding, a court held nonarbitrable a claim that certain employees who engaged in a strike had been singled out for severe punishment and disparate treatment.[17] The contract provided that there would be no right to arbitrate disciplinary actions taken against strikers. This exclusion prevailed over the right to challenge discipline action, which constituted disparate treatment.

If, however, the union is not challenging the ultimate right to take an action not subject to arbitration but is alleging a procedural violation of another clause that is subject to arbitration and requires notice and discussion before initiation of the action, the dispute has been held arbitrable.[18]

When there is no dispute over the meaning of the exclusionary language but there is a disagreement over whether the facts of a particular situation make it subject to the exclusionary language, the arbitrator is to resolve the dispute. For example, in a situation where there is no right to grieve disciplinary action taken against strikers but where the union argues that the discharged employees had not participated in a strike, the court held that it was for the arbitrator to determine whether or not the employees engaged in a strike.[19]

---

17. District 50, UAW v. Chris-Craft Corp., 385 F.2d 946, 67 L.R.R.M. 2124 (6th Cir. 1967).

18. International Ass'n of Machinists and Aerospace Workers v. General Electric Co., 406 F.2d 1046, 70 L.R.R.M. 2477 (2d Cir. 1969).

19. Sam Kane Packing v. Meat Cutters, 477 F.2d 1128, 83 L.R.R.M. 2298 (5th Cir. 1973).

In another case, the arbitrator was proscribed by the contract from preventing the employer from creating new jobs. The court held that the employer was required to arbitrate because there was a dispute of fact over whether or not the introduction of a conveyor created new jobs.[20] In a case in which the contract precluded arbitration of an issue that had previously been arbitrated, the court, determining that it was for the arbitrator to decide the scope and effect of the prior award, held the matter arbitrable.[21]

Under a contract that specifically excluded from arbitration matters related to the exercise of management rights, one of the management rights was to discharge for just cause. When a discharged employee grieved, the court concluded that until the discharge is determined to be for just cause the exclusionary clause does not apply, and it found the matter arbitrable.[22]

Notice that if a broad action by management is not reviewable in arbitration, a challenge to such action is usually not arbitrable. If, however, an action based on a particular reason or motivation is excluded from arbitration, it is for the arbitrator to determine the motivating factor. Thus, when an employer had the right to terminate employees for lack of work or other proper reasons, the union's charge that the terminations constituted a lockout in violation of the contract was held arbitrable.[23] The issue of whether there was a proper reason for the terminations was for the arbitrator to resolve.

---

20. Radiator Corp. v. Operative Potters, 358 F.2d 455, 61 L.R.R.M. 2664 (6th Cir. 1966).

21. Electric Workers, IUE, Local 103 v. RCA Corp., 516 F.2d 1336, 89 L.R.R.M. 2487 (3d Cir. 1975).

22. Johnston-Tombigbee Mfg. Co. v. Local 2462, 596 F.2d 126, 101 L.R.R.M. 2486 (5th Cir. 1979).

23. Local 198, Rubber Workers v. Interco., Inc., 415 F.2d 1208, 72 L.R.R.M. 2377 (8th Cir. 1969).

A very difficult issue is the determination of whether the court or arbitrator should interpret exclusionary language if there is a dispute over the nature and extent of that language. The typical disagreement over whether a particular dispute comes within the scope of the arbitration clause involves a contract that does not contain exclusionary language. In this situation, the Trilogy holds that the presumption of arbitrability applies. The court will require arbitration unless it can be shown with positive assurance that the matter is not arbitrable.

In the typical cases, the court is not passing on the underlying basis of the objection to arbitration; the arbitrator will be presented that precise question. Furthermore, the determination of arbitrability has no bearing on the arbitrator's ultimate decision on the merits. Suppose, for instance, an employer closes its plant the first two weeks in July and requires all employees to take vacation time during that period. The union grieves, alleging a violation of the vacation clause of the collective bargaining agreement. Claiming that the contract only provides the number of vacation days but does not deal with the right to designate the vacation period, the employer challenges arbitrability. The court concludes that the contract is susceptible to an interpretation sustaining the union and holds the grievance to be arbitrable. The issue is then presented to the arbitrator on its merits. Although the employer lost the arbitrability challenge, the arbitrator will still resolve the underlying dispute. The issue before the arbitrator is whether the contract prevents the employer from designating the vacation period.

The court's limited function in these cases makes sense because the underlying issue the court is declining to resolve will be resolved by the arbitrator on the basis of the nature and extent of the contract language which is subject to arbitration. The parties have agreed that the arbitrator should make that determination.

There is a significant distinction between a dispute over a substantive portion of the contract and a dispute over the meaning of exclusionary language in the grievance definition. This is because if the court has interpreted the exclusionary language in such a manner to hold the dispute arbitrable, the arbitrator is to determine the merits of the grievance and not to interpret the disputed exclusionary language. The underlying issue in the arbitrability challenge is the meaning of the exclusionary language, but that issue will not be submitted to the arbitrator. This is not contract language the parties have agreed to have interpreted by an arbitrator. The court should accept and evaluate any relevant evidence that assists in that contract interpretation, including bargaining history, past practice, and the meaning of other portions of the contract.

Given the court's role as the ultimate interpreter of the meaning of the exclusionary language, it is inappropriate to apply a presumption of arbitrability and deny arbitration only if it can be shown with positive assurance that the dispute is not arbitrable. In this situation, there is no justification to permit arbitration solely for therapeutic value. But, given the federal preference for arbitration and the Supreme Court's stated requirement of forceful evidence to preclude arbitration, there is a substantial burden of proof on the party challenging arbitrability. The first of the two case decisions that follow is commendable because it demonstrates the extensive evidence necessary to interpret the exclusionary language, but in the second the court does not seriously attempt to interpret the exclusionary language. In *Local 81* v. *Western Electric*, it was not clear whether the exclusionary language that barred arbitration over a merit increase also barred review of the rating system. The court of appeals, therefore, ordered a district court hearing to permit evidence on bargaining history.[24]

In *International Ass'n of Machinists and Aerospace Workers* v. *General Electric,* the collective bargaining agreement excluded from arbitration the company's right to schedule shutdowns. One of the arbitrability issues was the question of whether shutdowns included the closing of the company for one day for fewer than all the employees. Without an extensive discussion of the merits, the interpretation of the term *shutdown*, the court held the matter arbitrable because it could not be said with positive assurance that the arbitration clause is not susceptible of covering the grievance.[25]

---

24. 508 F.2d 106, 88 L.R.R.M. 2081 (7th Cir. 1974).

25. General Electric, *supra* note 18.

# 5.

## Miscellaneous Defenses

THIS CHAPTER discusses some defenses that may be raised as the basis of an objection to proceeding before the arbitrator on the merits of the grievance. Only the first defense discussed, procedural arbitrability, is frequently raised. Although seldom raised, the other defenses are included in order to further the understanding of potential arbitrability challenges and the role of the court in determining arbitrability.

The cases in which these defenses have arisen do not rely on a stated presumption of arbitrability. As in any contract dispute, however, the burden of proof rests on the party objecting to proceeding on the merits while acknowledging the existence of a contract he or she signed.

### Procedural Arbitrability

If raised in court, procedural arbitrability issues, questions of whether the contractual procedure has been followed, have been routinely held to be for the arbitrator to resolve.[1] This precedent includes claims that the procedural prerequi-

---

1. John Wiley and Sons v. Livingston, 376 U.S. 543, 55 L.R.R.M. 2769 (1964).

site steps to arbitration were not followed or that they were not completed in a timely fashion.[2]

There are two main reasons the courts have determined procedural arbitrability issues are for the arbitrator. First, questions relating to compliance with the contract grievance procedure are themselves considered questions of contract interpretation, which the parties agreed the arbitrator should resolve.[3] Second, the procedural issue is often intertwined with the substantive issue. Questions such as Was the grievance timely filed?, Is the grievance sought to be arbitrated the same as the grievance raised in the earlier steps of the grievance procedure?, and Are there equitable reasons to excuse untimeliness? often compel an in-depth analysis of the substantive issue. To avoid duplicative litigation, the courts defer to the arbitrator. It is desirable to have the arbitrator who is selected to resolve the substantive issue also resolve the entwined procedural issue. The alternative would be for the court to resolve both the procedural and substantive issues, but that would conflict with the parties' agreement to arbitrate substantive disputes.

## Fraud and Duress

Questions relating to the validity of the contract are for the court.

> It is our view that [the appellant's] attack upon the validity of the underlying contract goes to the heart of whether there is anything to arbitrate—not just what there is to arbitrate—and thus poses a legal question for the court rather than

2. UMW, District 50, Local 12934 v. Dow Corning Corp., 459 F.2d 221, 80 L.R.R.M. 2218 (6th Cir. 1972).

3. Radio Corp. v. Association of Professional Engineering Personnel, 291 F.2d 105, 48 L.R.R.M. 2270 (3d Cir. 1961).

arbitrator. The arbitrator who derives his power solely from the contract cannot hold that charter to be legally ineffective.[4]

## Laches

While procedural arbitrability concerns intrinsic untimeliness relating to the contract requirements, laches concerns extrinsic untimeliness and relates to basic equity. In order to prevail, the party seeking to charge the other side with laches must not only establish unexplained or inexcusable delay but must also demonstrate resulting prejudice or injury.

In several decisions, courts of appeals have reached divergent results as to the proper forum in which to resolve the issue of laches. One court found that the arbitrator is in the best position to resolve this issue and that any other decision would afford the employer two bites at the apple because the same proof of bargaining history was required in each forum.[5] Another court concluded that deciding a question of laches did not constitute resolving a question of contract interpretation and found the matter within the court's province.[6] This decision was reversed by the Supreme Court on the grounds that the parties agreed to a broad grievance definition ("any dispute"), which encompassed the issue of laches, and that therefore the issue should have been presented to the arbitrator.[7] The Supreme Court did not state

4. ILGWU v. Ashland Industries, Inc., 488 F.2d 641, 644, 85 L.R.R.M. 2319, 2320 (5th Cir. 1974).

5. Lodge 1327, IAM v. Fraser & Johnston Co., 454 F.2d 88, 79 L.R.R.M. 2118 (9th Cir. 1971).

6. International Union of Operating Engineers, Local 150 v. Flair Builders, Inc., 440 F.2d 557, 76 L.R.R.M. 2595 (7th Cir. 1971).

7. International Union of Operating Engineers, Local 150 v. Flair Builders, Inc., 406 U.S. 487, 80 L.R.R.M. 2441 (1972).

any dictum to indicate how the case would have been resolved had the grievance definition been limited to contract interpretation.

## Res Judicata and Stare Decisis

The doctrine of *res judicata,* which means a party cannot be required to relitigate the same case twice, applies to labor arbitrations at least to the extent that a party may not relitigate in court the same matter brought to arbitration.[8] But it is the function of the arbitrator, not the court, to determine if the identical issue had been the subject of a previous arbitration.[9] In accordance is the decision holding that it is for the arbitrator to resolve whether the parties are bound by their prior arbitration if there is an arguable material difference in the cases.[10] This approach implies that, given specific, limited facts, the court would apply *res judicata* to a subsequent arbitration. The same violation involving a different employee, however, does not provide a basis for the application of *res judicata,*[11] nor does an attempt to arbitrate the interpretation of a contract clause that was the subject of an arbitration during the term of the previous contract.[12]

Even when the contract provided that the same issue

---

8. Little Six Corp. v. United Mine Workers of America, Local 8332, 701 F.2d 26, 112 L.R.R.M. 2922 (4th Cir. 1983).

9. Local 103 of Int'l Union of Elec. Radio and Mach. Workers v. RCA Corp., 516 F.2d 1336, 89 L.R.R.M. 2487 (3d Cir. 1975); Little Six Corp., *supra* note 8.

10. Boston Shipping Ass'n v. International Longshoremen's Ass'n, 659 F.2d 1, 108 L.R.R.M. 2449 (1st Cir. 1981).

11. Local Lodge 1617 v. Associated Transport, Inc., 92 L.R.R.M. 2342 (DC NC 1976).

12. Westinghouse Elevators of Puerto Rico, Inc. v. S.I.U. de Puerto Rico, 583 F.2d 1184, 99 L.R.R.M. 2651 (1st Cir. 1978).

shall not be the subject of arbitration more than once, the court held that the arbitrator should interpret and apply the rearbitration provision.[13]

Nevertheless, two cases suggest that *res judicata* might not be an acceptable basis to enjoin an arbitration. In these cases, the courts have held that the question of the preclusive effect of a prior arbitration award is for the arbitrator.[14]

The arbitrator is not required to abide by the doctrine of *stare decisis,* which requires that one tribunal follow the decision of another. The weight to be afforded a prior arbitration award (not necessarily involving the same parties or an identical issue) is within the discretion of the arbitrator.

## Repudiation or Abandonment

A repudiation or abandonment of a contract occurs when a party manifests an intention not to perform contractual obligations. Although this doctrine may apply to arbitration cases, the Supreme Court held that the union's violation of the no-strike clause does not constitute a repudiation of the contract, which would have thereby relieved the employer of his or her duty to arbitrate.[15]

## Mootness

Although the court will not direct arbitration of a dispute that is moot, if alleged wrongful behavior can reasonably be expected to recur, the case will be ordered to arbitration. In one case, after successfully bidding for a position in another

---

13. RCA, *supra* note 9.

14. Little Six Corp., *supra* note 8; New Orleans S.S. Ass'n v. General Longshore Workers, 626 F.2d 455, 105 L.R.R.M. 2539 (5th Cir. 1980).

15. Local Union No. 721 v. Needham Packing Co., 376 U.S. 247, 55 L.R.R.M. 2480 (1964).

facility, an employee refused to change his residence despite a company rule requiring such a change. Before the arbitration, the employee was promoted and had no desire to pursue his grievance. The court held that the real dispute was over the validity of the residency rule, and was not moot because the issue was likely to come up again.[16]

---

16. Electrical Workers, IBEW v. Puget Sound Power & Light Co., 506 F.2d 523, 87 L.R.R.M. 3158 (9th Cir. 1974).

# 6.

# Jurisdictional Conflict

TWO TYPES of jurisdictional questions frequently arise in labor arbitration. The first type arises when, in addition to the contract right to arbitrate the dispute, there is a statutory right to redress through a government tribunal, for instance, the National Labor Relations Board (NLRB) and antidiscrimination agencies such as the Equal Employment Opportunity Commission (EEOC). The second type of jurisdictional conflict occurs when a party seeks to have contract rights litigated in a forum other than arbitration. This usually happens when court action is instituted under section 301 of the Labor-Management Relations Act to enforce rights contained in the collective bargaining agreement.

## Identical Statutory and Contractual Rights

### EEOC Jurisdictional Conflict
In a very well-known case, *Alexander* v. *Gardner-Denver,* the Supreme Court decided that the statutory right of an individual to bring an action under Title VII of the Civil Rights Act of 1964 may not be waived by a union in a collective

bargaining agreement.[1] Therefore, even when an identical right is contained in the contract and the union, on behalf of the employees, has obtained an arbitration award covering the dispute, an employee may file a charge raising the same issue with the EEOC. An interesting question is if, to avoid duplicate litigation, a contract may provide arbitration but specifically exclude the processing of a claim that has been raised before the EEOC.

Recently, the Court rejected an employer's argument that public policy dictated that an arbitrator's holding of liability under the collective bargaining agreement should be vacated.[2] The employer had voluntarily entered into an EEOC conciliation agreement that conflicted with the layoff provision of its collective bargaining agreement. The court held that, absent a judical determination, neither the EEOC nor the employer could alter the collective bargaining agreement without the union's consent, and it concluded that no public policy would be violated by enforcing the arbitration award.

### Fair Labor Standards Act
In a decision similar to *Alexander* v. *Gardner-Denver,* the Supreme Court ruled that an arbitration award does not act as a waiver of an employee's right to a trial de novo of the employee's claim under the Fair Labor Standards Act.[3] Therefore, even though a dispute was submitted to arbitration and an award had been rendered, the alleged statutory violation could still be raised in court by the individual employee.

---

1. 415 U.S. 36, 7 Fair Empl. Prac. Cas. 81 (1974).

2. W. R. Grace v. Local Union 759, 203 S.Ct. 2177, 113 L.R.R.M. 2641 (1983).

3. Barrentine v. Arkansas–Best Freight System, Inc., 450 U.S. 728, 24 Wage & Hour Cas. 1284 (1981).

## NLRB Jurisdictional Conflict

The mere fact that another tribunal may have jurisdiction over the underlying issue does not necessarily restrict or revoke the concomitant jurisdiction of the arbitrator. The NLRB has the authority to determine the appropriateness of bargaining units and may occasionally clarify prior rulings. Thus, disputes over which union's contract applies to a specific job may be resolved by the NLRB. But despite the fact that the dispute may ultimately be resolved by the NLRB and despite the fact that perhaps not all parties to the dispute will be bound by the arbitrator's award, the dispute will not be declared nonarbitrable merely because the question can be raised before the NLRB.[4] Thus, in cases in which the NLRB has not yet exercised its jurisdiction and may never do so, the claim may be brought to the arbitrator under the contract arbitration provision.[5] When the parties' contract does not cover the dispute, the issue will be held nonarbitrable even though the parties have the power to include such items in their contract.[6]

In a case where the dispute had been raised before the NLRB, the court held the issue arbitrable because the NLRB might still defer. The remedy requested went beyond what could be expected from the NLRB and any other decision would encourage dilatory tactics.[7] In another case, although the union filed an unfair labor practice charge that the employer interfered with its statutory rights when it

---

4. Carey v. Westinghouse Electric Corp., 375 U.S. 261, 55 L.R.R.M. 2042 (1964).

5. UMW, District 50, Local 12934 v. Dow Corning Corp., 459 F.2d 221, 80 L.R.R.M. 2218 (6th Cir. 1972).

6. Operating Engineers, Local 279 v. Sid Richardson Carbon Co., 471 F.2d 1175, 82 L.R.R.M. 2403 (5th Cir. 1973).

7. Lodge 1327, IAM v. Fraser & Johnston Co., 454 F.2d 88, 79 L.R.R.M. 2118 (9th Cir. 1971).

suspended an employee, the employer's right to submit that matter to arbitration was upheld by the court.[8]

"Once the Board has acted, either before or after the arbitrator's award, the Board's order overrides the arbitrator's decision." Thus when an arbitrator ordered reimbursement to make an employee whole for lost wages and benefits caused by the violation of contract, the NLRB's subsequent determination that another union's contract applied vitiated the arbitration award.[9] The court held that the first union's contract never applied to the employees involved and that the company could not be liable for breach of that contract when it would have been in violation of the law if it applied the contract. The application of one union's contract to employees in a unit certified to another union would constitute an unfair labor practice.

## Litigation of Contract Rights in Another Forum

A suit in court to enforce a right contained in a labor contract will be dismissed if the matter has been litigated through the arbitration process or a party has not exhausted its contractual right to arbitrate the dispute. Because it is clearly the court's policy to avoid dual litigation, the arbitration process will usually prevail over a court suit. For example, when the contract provides that the employer may arbitrate its claim for damages for violation of the no-strike clause, a court action seeking damages will be dismissed.

When an employee establishes that the union has not represented him or her fairly, the employee will be permit-

---

8. United Aircraft Corp. v. Canel Lodge 700, 436 F.2d 1, 76 L.R.R.M. 2111 (2d Cir. 1970).

9. Local 7-210 v. Union Tank Car Co., 475 F.2d 194, 199, 82 L.R.R.M. 2823, 2827 (7th Cir. 1973).

ted to institute a court suit pursuant to section 301 of the Labor-Management Relations Act, even though the union opted not to submit the dispute to arbitration or even though an arbitration award has already been issued. The award will not be considered binding on the individual.

A recent decision held that the employer was required to use the arbitration clause of the contract where that clause was not found to exclude with "positive assurance" employer-initiated grievances. [10]

---

10. Eberle Tanning Co. v. Food & Commercial Workers, Sec. 63L, 682 F.2d 430, 110 L.R.R.M. 3136 (1982).

# 7.

## The Arbitrator's Authority

GENERALLY, ARBITRABILITY challenges that may have been raised in court before the commencement of the arbitration may also be raised in court after the issuance of an arbitration award. The party challenging arbitrability will have to ensure that his or her participation in the arbitration process does not constitute a waiver of his or her right to object to arbitrability. These arbitrability challenges raised after the award are dealt with in the same manner as those raised before arbitration commences. Thus, an employer's argument that, because he or she participated in the arbitration, the court should no longer impose a preference for arbitration and should grant a more extensive review of arbitrability, was found to be unpersuasive.[1]

This chapter is devoted to the enforceability of an arbitration award when the basis of a challenge relates to a decision of the arbitrator. By definition, these challenges could not have been raised before the arbitration hearing, while challenges discussed in other chapters could have.

---

1. International Association of Machinists and Aerospace Workers, District 776 v. Texas Steel Co., 538 F.2d 1116, 93 L.R.R.M. 2285 (5th Cir. 1976).

# Basis for Vacating an Award

A court will vacate an arbitration award if the party attacking the award establishes the existence of one of the statutory bases for vacating the award. The federal law (U.S.C. 9 §10) provides grounds for vacating awards:

a) Where the award was procured by corruption, fraud, or undue means.

b) Where there was evident partiality or corruption in the arbitrators, or either of them.

c) Where the arbitrators were guilty of misconduct in refusing to hear evidence pertinent and material to the controversy; or of any other misbehavior by which the rights of any party have been prejudiced.

d) Where the arbitrators exceeded their powers, or so imperfectly executed them that a mutual, final, and definite award upon the subject matter submitted was not made.

e) Where an award is vacated and the time within which the agreement required the award to be made has not expired the court may, in its discretion, direct a rehearing by the arbitrators.

Claims that the arbitrator did not have jurisdiction to hear the case or that the arbitrator's award exceeded his or her scope of authority would fall within subsection (d) of the law. If the agreement contains a provision covering an area in which the parties lack the capacity to make a binding agreement, known as a prohibited bargaining subject (e.g., agreeing to pay less than the minimum wage), the court will vacate an award enforcing the provision. The wording of either the arbitration clause of the contract or the submission agreement is irrelevant in this situation. The arbitrator's authority is limited by the legal capacity of the parties under whose contract he or she is functioning. The parties cannot delegate to the arbitrator authority that they do not possess.

## Scope of Review of an Arbitration Award

The role of the court in reviewing the arbitrator's decision is narrowly circumscribed. Doubts are resolved in favor of enforcement of the award.[2] Usually, the award will be affirmed if it can be derived in any rational way from the agreement; it will be reversed only if there is a manifest disregard for the principles of contract interpretation and the common law of the shop.[3] Where the arbitration award is clearly based upon sources outside the contract, the award will be vacated. In *Steelworkers* v. *Enterprise Wheel and Car Co.,* the Supreme Court said,

> [the arbitrator] may, of course, look for guidance from many sources, yet his award is legitimate only so long as it draws its essence from the collective bargaining agreement. When the arbitrator's words manifest an infidelity to this obligation, courts have no choice but to refuse enforcement of the award.[4]

Thus, the courts will review the award to determine whether the arbitrator exceeded his or her authority as provided for in the collective bargaining agreement.

## Acceptance of Arbitrator Judgment

The generally narrow role of the court and the enormous reliance on the arbitrator's judgment apply to interpretations of the contract, identification of the common law of the shop, findings of fact, and findings of law.

    The court does not substitute its interpretation of the

---

2. United Steelworkers of America v. Warrior & Gulf Navigation Co., 363 U.S. 574, 46 L.R.R.M. 2416 (1960).

3. Ludwig Honold Mfg. Co. v. Fletcher, 405 F.2d 1123, 70 L.R.R.M. 2368 (3d Cir. 1969); Electrical Workers, IUE v. Peerless Pressed Metal Corp. 489 F.2d 768, 82 L.R.R.M. 3089 (1st Cir. 1973).

4. 363 U.S. 593, 597, 46 L.R.R.M. 2423, 2425 (1960).

contract for that of the arbitrator's.[5] This is affirmed by the Supreme Court:

> So far as the arbitrator's decision concerns construction of the contract, the courts have no business overruling him because their interpretation of the contract is different than his.[6]

The object of the federal labor law is to encourage resolution of labor dispute through labor arbitration. In order to further this goal, the courts usually will not review the legal accuracy of the arbitrator's findings.[7] Thus an arbitrator's award is more binding (less subject to review and possible overturning) than the decision of a court of initial jurisdiction. One court decision, however, offers a significant caveat.

> An arbitrator's award will not be vacated even though the arbitrator may have made, in the eyes of judges, errors of fact and law, unless it compels the violation of law or conduct contrary to accepted public policy.[8]

To the extent an award is challenged because it requires an action that contravenes public policy or compels the violation of law, the court will not limit its review or defer to the findings of the arbitrator.

## Stipulation of the Issue

While the authority of the arbitrator is generally determined by the scope of the arbitration clause, the parties'

---

5. Asbestos Workers, Local 66 v. Lena Lee Corp., 489 F.2d 1032, 85 L.R.R.M. 2446 (5th Cir. 1974).

6. Enterprise Wheel, *supra* note 4, at 599.

7. Meat Cutters, Local 540 v. Neuhoff Bros. Packers, Inc., 481 F.2d 817, 83 L.R.R.M. 2026, 2028 (5th Cir. 1969)).

8. Washington-Baltimore Newspaper Guild, Local 35 v. The Washington Post Co., 442 F.2d 1234, 1239, 76 L.R.R.M. 2274, 2278 (DC Cir. 1971) (citing Gulf States Telephone Co. v. Local 1692, IBEW, 416 F.2d 198, 210, 72 L.R.R.M. 2026, 2028 (5th Cir. 1969).

submission to the arbitrator also has a significant bearing on the scope of the arbitrator's authority. The arbitration clause in the contract constitutes the parties' agreement as to what may be arbitrated under the contract. The parties can agree to arbitrate a dispute even though they have no arbitration clause in the contract or even no contract. A contract to arbitrate will be enforced whether it is broad, extends over a number of years, and is incorporated in a larger agreement or whether it is confined to one specific dispute.

The parties' stipulation of the issue may vary from the arbitration clause. It is possible for the parties to use their submission agreement in a particular case to expand or restrict the general powers of an arbitrator defined by their contract.[9] For example, assume that a contract contained a provision requiring that all discipline be imposed only for just cause and stating that discipline imposed for violation of the no-strike clause would not be subject to the grievance and arbitration provision. Also assume that an employee who was disciplined for engaging in a prohibited strike claimed he or she received disparate treatment, and the parties submitted to an arbitrator the issue, "Was the employee disciplined for just cause? If not, what shall be the remedy?" In this hypothetical situation, the arbitrator would have the authority to determine whether there existed just cause for the discipline because the employer waived its right to challenge arbitrability by submitting the grievance on its merits to the arbitrator. The specific submission agreement would supercede the general contractual agreement.

There would be a different result if the parties agreed that the issue before the arbitrator would be "What shall be the disposition of the grievance?" With this submission, no

---

9. Ficek v. Southern Pacific Co., 338 F.2d 655, 57 L.R.R.M. 2573 (9th Cir. 1964).

waiver of the right to raise an arbitrability issue can be implied. The submission to the arbitrator would include the issue of arbitrability, which then could be raised to the arbitrator during the arbitration proceedings.

It is common for the parties to submit to the arbitrator substantive arbitrability issues that otherwise would be resolved in court. [10] Cost saving, expediency, and the expertise of the arbitrator are reasons for choosing to present such issues to the arbitrator.

The intent to modify the contract will not be lightly inferred. The courts will probably be reluctant to hold that the submission agreement or stipulation of the issue modifies the contract, and there will probably be a substantial burden on a party urging this contention. But if it is determined that the parties did agree to have the arbitrator resolve the arbitrability issue, any court review of the arbitrator's decision on arbitrability should be as circumspect as its review of the arbitrator's decision on the merits of the grievance.

## No Agreement on the Issue

A frequent question is, May the arbitrator hear a case in which the parties do not agree upon the specific issue to be submitted? If the moving party's framing of the issue is objectionable to the respondent for either legitimate or arbitrary reasons, may the arbitrator proceed with the case? The answer is yes, with the caveat that the arbitrator's authority cannot be expanded by the way that he or she frames the issue. In most cases in which the parties cannot agree on the framing of the issue, that task is delegated to the arbitrator,

---

10. Metal Products Workers v. Torrington Co., 358 F.2d 103, 62 L.R.R.M. 2011 (2d Cir. 1966).

and the framing of the issue is viewed as an analysis and articulation of the nature of the dispute rather than a determination of the arbitrator's jurisdiction.

If the dispute over the framing of the issue represents a serious and substantial disagreement over the arbitrator's jurisdiction, the arbitrator may grant a continuance to permit a party to raise in court its objection to the wording of the issue that the opposing side wishes to submit to the arbitrator. But if the expediency of the hearing is itself an important consideration, the arbitrator may refuse a continuance. Once the arbitrator has been properly appointed, any party declining or refusing to participate in the arbitration process does so at the risk of having the process continued *ex parte*. Although the absent party may challenge in court the outcome of the arbitration subsequent to the award being issued, if this claim is rejected the party would have relinquished the right to participate in the arbitration. An *ex parte* arbitration proceeding is not invalidated because a party refused to participate in the hearing or because a party made a special appearance to challenge the arbitrator's jurisdiction.

## Explanation by the Arbitrator

Although an arbitrator is not required to explain the basis of his or her award and the court encourages the arbitrator to explain the reasons, if the explanation discloses or divulges that the award had an improper basis, the award will be vacated.[11]

Therefore, where the contract required an employee to positively establish that the performance of a task would create a serious health hazard, the court vacated the arbitra-

---

11. Enterprise Wheel, *supra* note 4, at 597.

tor's award, which acknowledged that the employee had not sustained this burden but harbored only good faith doubts of a health hazard.[12]

## Award's Consistency with the Contract

When the arbitration award is consistent with the clear meaning, or at least a reasonable interpretation, of the contract provision that is the crux of the parties' dispute, the court review will be perfunctory, and the court will not substitute its interpretation for that of the arbitrator's.

If the contract language is obviously ambiguous, virtually any interpretation by an arbitrator will have to be considered derived from the contract language and, therefore, within the arbitrator's authority to render.

> If the arbitrator's award has deviated from the plain meaning of a labor contract provision, it must find support in the contract itself or in prior practices, demonstrating relaxation of the literal language.[13]

What may appear to be clear contract language may undertake a significantly different meaning in the light of the rest of the contract, the practice of the parties, and the bargaining history of specific contract items.

In *Machinists* v. *Modern Air Transportation, Inc.*, the arbitrator ruled that the contract language that referred to work "customarily" contracted out in fact related to work that had been exclusively contracted out. The court of appeals upheld the arbitrator's award.[14] It stated the general rules that an arbitration award without foundation in reason

---

12. Magnavox Co. v. Electrical Workers, 410 F.2d 388, 71 L.R.R.M. 2049 (6th Cir. 1969).

13. NF&M Corp. v. United Steelworkers of America, 524 F.2d 756, 90 L.R.R.M. 2947 (3d Cir. 1975).

14. 495 F.2d 1241, 86 L.R.R.M. 2886 (5th Cir. 1974).

or fact is tantamount to an award that exceeds the arbitrator's authority and that the award must be in some logical way derived from the wording or purpose of the contract. In this case, however, the court of appeals found that the district court usurped the arbitrator's function of contract interpretation.

> Analyzing the arbitrator's reasoning, he performed the traditional function of one delegated to resolve contractual disputes. He interpreted and gave meaning (exclusively) to an ambiguous (customarily) contract term in light of the other provisions and purposes of the contract. His award was well founded in the "essence" of, and more than "rationally inferable" from its letter and purpose of, the collective bargaining agreement. . . . Neither the district court nor we have any business overruling him because [our] interpretation of the contract is different from his.[15]

Contrast the *Modern Air Transportation* case with *Monongahela Power Co.* v. *IBEW*, in which the contract provided that the employer had the "unqualified" right to discharge or discipline employees who engaged in a strike in violation of the no-strike clause.[16] The arbitrator held that the employees engaged in a violation of the no-strike clause. While upholding the employer's decision to stagger disciplinary suspensions because of the critical need to maintain continuous service, the award provided the suspensions must be served within sixty days. The court vacated that portion of the award that required the employer to have the suspensions served within sixty days.

> The powers of an arbitrator are not unlimited. He derives his authority from and is bound by the terms of the contract from which he draws his authority; and while he may of course look for guidance from many sources, yet his award is legitimate only so long as it draws its essence from the collective bargaining agreement. His function is confined to the interpreta-

---

15. *Id.* at 1245.

16. 566 F.2d 1196, 91 L.R.R.M. 2583 (4th Cir. 1976).

tion and application of the collective bargaining agreement under which he acts and, while he may give his own construction to ambiguous language, he is without any authority to disregard or modify plain and unambiguous provisions.[17]

The *Modern Air Transportation* and *Monongahela* decisions seem consistent. In the former case, the arbitrator stated no basis, and the court could find no basis, to interpret a contract provision in any way other than its literal meaning. In the latter case, the arbitrator disclosed a proper basis for interpreting a contract provision in a certain manner.

If the award is not consistent with the plain meaning of the contract provision and the arbitrator does not express the basis for the award, the court will review the record to ascertain whether there is support for the award. Finding any there, the court will affirm the award even though the arbitrator did not expressly rely on that basis. But if no basis for the award is found, it will be vacated. In a case in which the court determined there was clear contract language, the contract provided that an employee who strikes in violation of the no-strike clause could be made the subject of discipline, including discharge. It also provided that employees would lose their seniority rights if discharged for cause and acknowledged the company had the sole responsibility for hiring. The arbitrator determined that the employees struck, that the company had the right to discharge, but that discharge coupled with an offer of reinstatement without seniority was punitive as violative of the contract. The court held that the arbitrator exceeded his powers when he varied from the express contract language, and it vacated the award.[18]

---

17. *Id.* at 1198.

18. Amanda Bent Bolt Co. v. Auto Workers, 541 F.2d 1277, 79 L.R.R.M. 2023 (6th Cir. 1971).

The most difficult questions about the proper standard of judical review of the validity of an award arise when the award is inconsistent with the apparent meaning of a contract provision and is based not on the consideration of other contract language but on factors outside the written contract, such as past practice or bargaining history. In this situation, the fine line between vacating an award that does not draw its essence from the contract and substituting the court's judgment for that of the arbitrator is difficult to discern. In *Steelworkers* v. *Enterprise,* the Supreme Court stated,

> The refusal of courts to review the merits of an arbitration award is the proper approach to arbitration under collective bargaining agreements. The federal policy of settling labor disputes by arbitration would be undermined if courts had the final say on the merits of the awards. [19]

Once it is determined that the evidence submitted to the arbitrator concerning relevant past practice or bargaining history supports the prevailing party, the court would be substituting its judgment for that of the arbitrator if it were to vacate the award. This is true regardless of the quantum of contrary evidence.

The Second Circuit's decision in *Torrington* v. *Metal Products Workers* is a case in which the court found no basis for an arbitration award. The case involved a grievance in which a union claimed that on election days employees should resume receiving up to one hour off with pay to vote, despite no reference to this paid time off in the contract. [20] Management had unilaterally instituted this practice many years before. But the court found determinative the fact that the practice had been unilaterally revoked under the prior contract and thus the union did not have the right to grieve the change. In addition, the court found it significant that

19. Enterprise Wheel, *supra* note 4, at 597.

20. 362 F.2d 677, 62 L.R.R.M. 2495 (2d Cir. 1966).

the benefit was discussed during negotiations over the current contract but omitted from that contract.

If the arbitrator had found that the practice did not in fact exist and the parties had no joint intent, expressed or implied, during the bargaining to resume the benefit, then there would be proper basis for the court to vacate the award. Under these circumstances, the court would not be substituting its findings for that of the arbitrator. It would be accepting the arbitrator's findings that no practice existed and no agreement was made to resume the benefit. Furthermore because the final agreement itself contained no provision remotely bearing on employee rights for time off on election day, the award would not have drawn its essence from the contract.

What makes the court's decision in *Torrington* difficult to analyze is that the arbitrator held the practice had not been discontinued. The employer's announcement that the benefit was rescinded occurred after the election day of the last year of the contract. The next election day fell before the consummation of a new contract and during a strike. While the majority of the court found that the arbitrator ignored the fact that the practice had ceased, the dissenter concluded that the arbitrator's finding should be accepted.

Apparently the Second Circuit is not comfortable with the majority's decision in *Torrington*.

> [W]e were concerned with the court's power to set aside an award when, according to the majority, the arbitrator had made clear that he did not rely on provisions of the contract.[21]

*Torrington* has been very narrowly construed by other circuits.

We think [*Torrington*] has to be very carefully confined lest,

---

21. F&M Schaffer Brewing Co. v. Local 49, Int'l Union of United Brewery, Flour, Cereal, Soft Drink and Distillery Workers of America, 420 F.2d 854, 856, 73 L.R.R.M. 2298, 2299 (2d Cir. 1970).

under the guise of the arbitrator not having "authority" to arrive at his ill-founded conclusions of law or fact, or both, the reviewing-enforcing court takes over the arbitrator's function.[22]

[*Torrington*] must not be read to justify the court resuming its traditional role of assaying the judical acceptability of the award had it been a court judgement.[23]

Consistent with our proper scope of review, we express no opinion as to whether our own construction of the contracts would coincide with that of the arbitrator. This is simply not our function. . . . Unless wholly unreasonable [the arbitrator's] is the interpretation which the courts must accept. To the extent *Torrington* may be read to authorize greater judicial intervention, we cannot accept it. Indeed, we are convinced the remarks of Judge Feinberg, dissenting in *Torrington,* more accurately describe the permissible scope of judicial involvement.[24]

Although a claim may be arbitrable because the court presumes the proper jurisdiction of the arbitrator, the ensuing arbitration award may nevertheless be vacated if it is rendered without proper basis.

## Ambiguous Award

The court will not enforce an award that is incomplete, ambiguous, or contradictory.[25] The court will not clarify an ambiguous award, but will remand it to the arbitrator for

---

22. Dallas Typographical Union No. 173 v. A. H. Belo Corp., 372 F.2d 577, 583, 64 L.R.R.M. 2491, 2494 (5th Cir. 1967).

23. Safeway Stores v. American Bakery & Confectionery Workers International Union, Local 111, 390 F.2d 79, 83, 67 L.R.R.M. 2646, 2648 (5th Cir. 1968).

24. Holly Sugar Corp. v. Distillery, Rectifying, Wine & Allied Workers International Union, 412 F.2d 899, 904, 71 L.R.R.M. 2841, 2845 (9th Cir. 1969).

25. Textron, Inc. v. Automobile Workers, Local 516, 500 F.2d 921, 86 L.R.R.M. 3240 (2d Cir. 1974).

clarification.[26] In a case in which the award was still contradictory after one remand, the court held,

> the purpose of arbitration is to resolve disputes not create new ones. An award which does not fulfill this purpose is unacceptable.[27]

The parties were instructed to agree on a new arbitrator or to have the court appoint one.

## Miscellaneous Contract Language

In some instances, the parties' contract language inhibits or discourages challenges to the arbitrator's authority. Note the obvious intent and impact of the following contract language:

> The Union and the Company, respectively, agree that there shall be no stoppage of work either by strike or lockout, and no intentional and concerted slowdown of work or production because of any dispute arising during the life of this Agreement or under the terms of this Agreement or any proposed modifications of amendments thereof; provided, however, that this Article XXIV shall not be binding upon one party if the other shall have failed or refused to comply with the grievance procedure hereunder or any decision or award of the arbitrators made thereunder.[28]

Sometimes the parties' grievance procedure contains a caveat that the arbitrator should not add to, subtract from, or modify the contract language. Although this may provide some satisfaction or solace to one or both parties, the language appears to have no effect on the arbitrator's jurisdiction to hear a case and authority to interpret the con-

---

26. Newspaper Guild, Local 25 v. Hearst Corp., 481 F.2d 821, 83 L.R.R.M. 2728 (5th Cir. 1973).

27. Textron, *supra* note 25, at 924.

28. Raytheon/IBEW, Local 1505 contract 1981–83.

tract.[29] For an award to be enforceable in court, it must draw its essence from the contract. Any award that does this cannot be found to add to, subtract from, or alter the contract. Although courts have relied on this language to explain their reasons for vacating arbitration awards,[30] there does not seem to be any difference in the court reviews of arbitration awards based on contracts that contain this caveat and those based on contracts that do not. The caveat, nevertheless, may influence the arbitrator's power to fashion a remedy.

## Procedural and Evidentiary Rulings

An arbitrator has great latitude in making procedural and evidentiary rulings. He or she does not have to adhere to the rules applying to federal courts but must at least provide the parties a fundamentally fair hearing.[31] Judicial review of the arbitration procedures is limited to extraordinary situations indicating abuse of arbitral power or exercise of power beyond the jurisdiction of the arbitrator.[32]

## Remedy

Assuming the arbitrator has the proper authority to hear the case and his or her resolution of the issue submitted is unassailable, a question may arise as to whether the remedy ordered exceeds the limits of the arbitrator's authority.

---

29. Western Iowa Pork Co. v. National Packinghouse and DairyWorkers, 366 F.2d 275, 63 L.R.R.M. 2187 (8th Cir. 1969).

30. Monongahela Power Co., *supra* note 16.

31. Textron, *supra* note 25.

32. Teamsters, Local 251 v. Narragansett Improvement Co., 503 F.2d 309, 87 L.R.R.M. 2279 (1st Cir. 1974).

The arbitrator is permitted wide latitude in fashioning a remedy. In each of the following cases, the arbitrator's award was upheld by the court. In one case, the employer was ordered to pay employees the wage increase that the arbitrator determined would have been agreed to if the employer, in violation of the contract, had not refused to negotiate.[33] The employer argued that it could be obligated only to bargain but could not be forced to agree to a particular wage increase. Since the union had been decertified after the violation, a bargaining order was eliminated as an appropriate remedy. The court enunciated the standard for review:

> Provided that his choice [of remedy] is not precluded by the arbitration provision under which he was acting, is adequately grounded in the contract, and is not arbitrary or capricious, we must uphold his action.[34]

In another case, the company had improperly refused to hire a person to operate certain machinery. The arbitrator required the company to pay to the union the salary an employee would have earned.[35]

Although the contract from which the arbitrator's authority is derived has expired, the remedy may be permitted to extend beyond the expiration date. In one of the Trilogy cases, *Steelworkers* v. *Enterprise Wheel and Car Corp.*, the court upheld an arbitrator's award of reinstatement and back pay that was rendered after the expiration of the contract under which the grievance had been brought.[36]

In another case, the arbitrator ordered back pay beyond

---

33. United Steelworkers of America v. United States Gypsum Co., 492 F.2d 713, 85 L.R.R.M. 2962 (5th Cir. 1974).

34. *Id.* at 730.

35. Bakery Workers v. Cotton Baking Co., 514 F.2d 1235, 89 L.R.R.M. 2665 (5th Cir. 1975).

36. *Supra* note 4.

the expiration of the contract and certification of a new union. The court noted,

> It is obvious that back pay lost because of improper discharge or suspension could exceed that which accrues to the date of termination of the collective bargaining agreement.[37]

The following caveats indicate some limitations on the arbitrator's broad and extensive authority to fashion a remedy:

1. The remedy must be limited to the issue submitted to the arbitrator. If, for instance, the issue submitted is whether the employer violated the contract when it denied overtime to employee X, the arbitrator would have no authority to determine the right or order a remedy as to employee Y.

2. The arbitrator may not order an employer to commit an unfair labor practice or an illegal act, such as negotiation with a decertified minority union.[38]

3. If the parties' submission does not include the issue of remedy, the arbitrator has no authority to order a remedy, although this issue may be raised to another arbitrator.[39]

4. While the arbitrator is permitted great latitude in determining how best to compensate a party for a loss incurred or occasioned by the other party's violation, the arbitrator has no authority to award punitive damages.[40]

---

37. ILWU Local 142 v. Land & Construction Co., 498 F.2d 201, 86 L.R.R.M. 2874 (9th Cir. 1974).

38. Glendale Mfg. Co. v. Local 520, ILGWU, 283 F.2d 936, 47 L.R.R.M. 2152 (4th Cir. 1960).

39. Retail Clerks, Local 782 v. Sav-On Groceries, 508 F.2d 500, 88 L.R.R.M. 3205 (10th Cir. 1975).

40. College Hall Fashions v. Clothing Workers, 408 F. Supp. 722, 91 L.R.R.M. 2608 (DC PA 1976).

5. Intervening events may limit the remedy to be ordered. Thus, an award of back pay and reinstatement should cease at the point when an employer goes out of business or all employees in the grievant's category are laid off. Similarly, an arbitrator's injunction against a strike becomes *functus officio* when the contract expires.[41]

---

41. Pacific Maritime Ass'n v. International Longshoremen's and Warehousemen's Union, 454 F.2d 262, 79 L.R.R.M. 2116 (9th Cir. 1971).

# 8.

# Public Sector Parties
# and Their Agreement

IT IS DIFFICULT to generalize about arbitrability in the public sector because each state has its own collective bargaining law, its own laws dealing with the operation of government services and public employment, and a series of court decisions interpreting and applying the various laws. While one state may prohibit the parties and the arbitrator from dealing with the many aspects covered by its civil service law,[1] another state may provide for the dominance of the contract, as interpreted by the arbitrator, over inconsistent provisions of its civil service law.[2]

The present discussion deals with arbitrability in New York and Massachusetts. These are two large industrial states that have had substantial experience under their respective collective bargaining statutes. New York's Taylor Law became effective in 1967,[3] and Massachusetts General

---

1. Mass. Gen. Laws ch. 150E § 7.

2. 1972 R.I. Public Law ch. 277.

3. New York Civil Service Law art. 14.

Law chapter 150E in 1974. These states do not necessarily typify how other states deal with specific arbitrability issues. The relevant laws and court decisions of each state must be examined to determine how arbitrability issues are resolved in the particular state. This discussion is intended to provide only the framework within which a particular state's laws and court decisions can be understood.

The most significant differences between the private and public sectors concern the authority of the parties and whether or not a presumption of arbitrability exists. The rule that the arbitrator cannot have any greater authority than that of the parties holds for both the private and public sectors. But because of the myriad potentially relevant statutes in the public sector, the application of this rule is much more frequent there. Therefore, the issues of arbitrability and the scope of the arbitrator's authority are much more frequently litigated in the public sector.

Since the initiation of statutory provision for collective bargaining in the private sector with the 1935 enactment of the National Labor Relations Act (Wagner Act), the courts have articulated the presumption of arbitrability. But the public sector does not automatically follow the private sector presumption of arbitrability. Since the public sector laws were enacted in the 1960s and 1970s, the determination of whether there is a presumption of arbitrability has not yet been fully resolved.[4]

---

4. It is interesting to note that the New York City law expressly favors final and binding arbitration for the resolution of grievances. New York City Collective Bargaining Law §1173−2.0. Resolution of arbitrability challenges constitutes a significant portion of the workload of the city's Office of Collective Bargaining, which also has jurisdiction over certification requests, unfair labor practice complaints, and issues of scope of bargaining. Its arbitrability decisions are almost never appealed to court.

## Employer

### Joint Employer

Identification of the employer in the public sector is complicated by the fact that in certain situations the person responsible for the day-to-day administration of an agency or department, including the hiring, firing, and assignment of employees, is not necessarily its chief fiscal officer. In the private sector, the administrative and fiscal officers report to the firm's chief executive officer, while in the public sector, the administrative officer may have statutory authority to act independently of the chief executive officer who has statutory responsibility for fiscal affairs.

New York State's Taylor Law makes specific reference to, and hence approval of, the joint employer concept.[5] Under the joint employer concept, a union negotiates simultaneously with the fiscal and the administrative officers, each official dealing only with those issues within the officer's statutory authority.

In Massachusetts, the Supreme Judicial Court has interpreted the public sector collective bargaining law to designate a single employer if at all possible, thus rejecting bifurcated negotiations as an undesirable format.[6] The Massachusetts legislature amended the state's public sector collective bargaining law, ch. 150E, in the three instances where it was believed that the statutory single employer created an unworkable bargaining structure: employees of constitutional officers (attorney general, state auditor, secretary of state, and state treasurer) were exempted from bargaining; the judiciary and lottery commission were designated

---

5. New York Civil Service Law art. 14, §200.6(b).

6. Labor Relations Commission v. Town of Natick, 369 Mass. 431, 339 N.E.2d 900 (1976).

as separate employers, but their collective bargaining contracts and those covering employees of public institutions of higher education were made subject to the governor's veto on fiscal matters.[7]

### Quasi-Public Employer
Another question concerning identification of the employer relates to quasi-public employers and independent authorities or agencies. The states' general collective bargaining laws may not extend coverage to such agencies, leaving the employees of such agencies with no rights to bargain under those laws. Some of these agencies may be covered by special statutes.[8]

# Is There a Binding Contract?

### Partial Invalidity
One of the defenses that may be raised to arbitration is that the contract as a whole is unenforceable.[9] It would be a most unusual situation for an entire collective bargaining agreement to be held invalid because one provision went beyond the authority of the parties and was unenforceable. The parties routinely provide a saving clause that specifically declares that the invalidity of one provision shall not affect the validity of the rest of the contract.

In two cases involving the validity of interest arbitra-

---

7. The amendments covering these employees are, respectively, Mass. St. 1975, ch. 689 §11; 1977, ch. 278 §2; 1977, ch. 937 §1; and 1976, ch. 480 §21, 1977 ch. 278 §4, 1977 ch. 937 §3.

8. Mass. St. 1962, ch. 760 §1.

9. Invalidity of a specific clause and the resulting unenforceability of that clause are different matters, which are discussed in Chapter 9, The Authority of Public Sector Parties.

tion awards, the court held partial invalidity of a contract determined by interest arbitration did not necessarily invalidate the entire award.[10] These cases involved the arbitrator's choice of final offer from those proposed by the parties. The court determined that the arbitrator's selection would not have been affected by the realization that the provision could not be implemented.

### Funding

The economic provisions of a contract may not become valid and enforceable until the necessary funds are appropriated to fund them. Both New York State and New York City laws provide that any contract provision requiring the enactment of a law for its implementation shall not be binding until the appropriate legislative body enacts such law.[11] Of course, this would be implicit in the absence of a specific statutory provision.

Massachusetts law provides that if the necessary funds are not appropriated, the economic items of an executed contract are to be returned to the parties for further bargaining.[12] The agreement on the noneconomic items would presumably be valid and enforceable even though there was not a complete contract. Of course, by conditioning their agreement, the parties could make the entire contract subject to fiscal approval, or they could agree to withhold implementation of any item until the entire contract is concluded.

It is not always a simple matter to determine whether a

---

10. Marlborough Firefighters v. City of Marlborough, 375 Mass. 593, 378 N.E.2d 437 (1978); Watertown Firefighters v. Town of Watertown, 376 Mass. 706, 383 N.E.2d 494 (1978).

11. New York State Civil Service Law §204a; New York City Collective Bargaining Law §1173−7.0c.

12. Mass. Gen. Laws ch. 150E §7(b).

contract has been funded. Furthermore, it may be unclear what effect the appropriation of some but not all the necessary funds would have. In the latter situation, the positions of the parties would no doubt be influenced by the source and effect, if any at all, of allocation of the additional funds necessary for full implementation.

In Massachusetts, the first two rounds of state contracts under the present law were funded by a fund established after negotiation of a contract covering the largest unit of employees and before the completion of negotiations with the smaller bargaining units. All contract costs were provided by either the fund or departments that were required to absorb certain costs within their budgets. Since no litigation resulted, many potential issues were never clarified, such as, Does the union that settled first have the right to have its contracts entirely funded with monies already appropriated for collective bargaining (even at the expense of depleting the funds available for subsequent settlements by other unions)? Does a union have the right to have its contract fully financed from the fund when it can establish that resort to an alternative source of money will result in layoffs or have some other negative effect on the employment relation?

A difficult question concerning the validity of a multi-year contract has recently been resolved by a decision of the Massachusetts Supreme Judicial Court.[13] The Massachusetts collective bargaining statute (ch. 150E §7(a)) specifically authorizes three-year contracts; however, before this decision, it had not been clear whether the validity of the contract was subject each year to the appropriation mechanism. It was also not clear if, after funds for the first year's

---

13. Boston Teachers Union, Local 66 v. School Committee of Boston, 386 Mass. 197, 434 N.E.2d 1258 (1982).

costs of a contract were appropriated by a legislture, a newly elected legislature would have the right to disapprove the contract by denying appropriations in subsequent years of the contract.

The Massachusetts Supreme Judicial Court ruled that once the first year's costs are appropriated, the contract is binding for its entire term (up to three years), and that the funds must be appropriated for subsequent years. In essence, the legislature gets only one opportunity to review the cost implications of a contract. The New York court held, in very strong language, that the deterioration of a public employer's fiscal position did not modify its commitments in an existing collective bargaining agreement.[14]

## Agreement to Arbitrate

Massachusetts collective bargaining law has a unique section (ch. 150E §8) that provides a statutory right to arbitrate a contract dispute, whether or not there is a specific agreement to arbitrate. The only prerequisite to arbitration is the existence of a collective bargaining agreement, and the Massachusetts Labor Relations Commission (MLRC) is given the authority to order arbitration of contract disputes involving contracts that do not contain an arbitration clause. Despite the statutory provision, nearly all public sector collective bargaining agreements contain a clause providing a multistep grievance-arbitration procedure.

Under another section of the law (ch. 150E §9A(b)), the MLRC ordered a public employer to arbitrate the dispute that prompted a work stoppage. This section requires the MLRC to investigate public sector strikes, which are

---

14. Board of Education v. Yonkers Federation of Teachers, 40 N.Y.2d 268, 386 N.Y.S.2d 657, 353 N.E.2d 569 (1976).

prohibited, and grants authority to the commission to set requirements to end the strike. The Supreme Judicial Court overturned the order, rejecting arguments that the law created a role for the MLRC to deal with strikes, which would be seriously diminished if the commission could not attempt to resolve the underlying dispute, and that private sector cases establish a linkage between injunctive relief from a strike and an order to arbitrate. The court held that chapter 150E "expresses no unrestrained preference for arbitration in the public employment situations" and that the MLRC has power only to set requirements to be complied with by the offending party.[15]

The court also found that the difference between the public and private sectors was significant:

> . . . although in the private sector a union's contractual waiver of its statutory right to strike may be presumptively tied to the employer's acceptance of binding arbitration for resolution of contract rights. . . , no similar linkage exists in the public sector cases.[16]

---

15. Director of the Division of Employee Relations v. Labor Relations Commission, 370 Mass. 162, 171, 346 N.E.2d 852, 858 (1976).

16. *Id.* at 173.

# 9.

## The Authority of
## Public Sector Parties

THE PRINCIPLE that the arbitrator can have no greater authority than the parties themselves is of major significance in the public sector. While the same principle applies in the private sector, its application is minimal. The reason for this difference is that in the public sector there are myriad statutes relating to the same subjects that in the private sector are unencumbered by statutory restraints.

In the public sector, many of the arbitrability challenges concern a party's objection to arbitration on the basis that it had no authority to enter into the contract. The determination of whether a subject is a mandatory, permissive, or prohibited bargaining subject is often made by a neutral agency subject to judicial review (these determinations are usually made as a result of a charge of refusal to bargain, an unfair labor practice). If the party (usually the employer) has no authority to commit itself to do something, then that subject is a *prohibited* bargaining subject, which the law does not permit the parties to bargain over. Because any agreement covering a prohibited subject is void and unenforceable, a party will not be required to arbitrate such a matter.

Any subject the parties are allowed to negotiate may be the basis of a contract provision, and such a provision is enforceable through arbitration.[1] This is true whether it is a *mandatory* subject, which the parties are required to bargain over upon request, or a *permissive* subject, which the parties are merely permitted to bargain over. The distinction between mandatory and permissive bargaining subjects is immaterial when determining arbitrability. So long as the party could have bargained over the subject, a contract provision containing it is susceptible to arbitral review.

Although some topics are wholly prohibited subjects, most often some aspects of the topic are prohibited and other aspects are not prohibited. For example, pensions are a prohibited bargaining subject in Massachusetts, and no aspect of it may be bargained.[2] In Massachusetts, while the type and extent of health insurance are not bargainable, the proportion of the employees' contribution is.[3]

When arguing that a grievance deals with a prohibited bargaining subject, parties often make the mistake of basing their argument on the requested remedy. The remedy requested by the party seeking to arbitrate is irrelevant in determining whether the grievance is arbitrable.[4] Arbitra-

1. Susquehanna Valley Central School Dist. v. Susquehanna Valley Teachers Ass'n, 37 N.Y.2d 614, 376 N.Y.S.2d 427, 339 N.E.2d 132 (1975) (citing West Irondequoit Teachers Ass'n v. Helsby, 35 N.Y.2d 46, 358 N.Y.S.2d 720, 315 N.E.2d 755 (1974) and Board of Education v. Associated Teachers of Huntington, 30 N.Y.2d 122, 331 N.Y.S.2d 17, 282 N.E.2d 109 (1972)).

2. Mass. Gen. Laws, ch. 150E §7(d); New York Civil Service Law art. 14.

3. School Committee of Holyoke v. Duprey, 8 Mass. App. Ct. 58, 391 N.E.2d 925 (1979).

4. Board of Education, Bellmore-Merrick Central High School District v. Bellmore-Merrick United Secondary Teachers, 39 N.Y.2d 167, 383 N.Y.S.2d 242, 347 N.E.2d 603 (1976).

tors are not restricted to the remedies requested by the parties. If it is possible for an arbitrator to grant some aspect of the claim (not necessarily the remedy requested), a stay of arbitration will not be granted. If the court can separate the prohibited subject from a permissible one, it will. If a single claim relates to matters both prohibited and permissive, the court will not assume that the arbitrator will go byond his or her authority. It will permit the arbitration,[5] but the arbitrator's award is reviewable to ensure that it does not exceed permissible bounds.

> [E]ven though the full scope of relief in precisely the form demanded by the teachers association might, if granted *in toto* by the arbitrator, ultimately lead to an award which would be subject to vacatur this consideration does not, standing alone, justify judicial interference with the arbitration process at this stage. The arbitrator's broad power to fashion appropriate relief may therefore not be presumed in advance to necessarily entail public policy conflicts discernable in the abstract of the courts. It follows that where the relief sought is broader than any enforceable remedy that may prospectively be granted but may also be adequately narrowed to encompass only procedural guarantees, as in these cases, a stay of arbitration on policy grounds is premature and unjustified.[6]

To determine whether a particular subject is a prohibited bargaining subject, one must balance the legislative intent and the underlying policy considerations of the general collective bargaining statute against that of the specific legislation dealing with the subject matter. The specialized legislation may be confined to state, city or town, or school district employees. It may relate to certain types of employees, such as police, fire fighters, or teachers. It may also re-

---

5. School Committee of Southbridge v. Brown, 375 Mass. 502, 377 N.E.2d 935 (1978).

6. Port Washington Union Free School District v. Port Washington Teachers Ass'n, 45 N.Y.2d 411, 418, 408 N.Y.S.2d 453, 456, 380 N.E.2d 280, 283 (1978).

late to particular benefits such as job security, health and welfare, or retirement.

The subject of the majority of court cases is educational policy. This is because the job duties of teachers directly affect the policy goals of the employers and because teachers are generally not covered by civil service law provisions that specifically delineate methods of selection, appointment, and promotion for other public sector employees. (Although teachers are covered by specialized statutes, these statutes do not restrict collective bargaining as much as the civil service statutes.)

Issues in law enforcement employment also generate a good deal of litigation. The courts have found that public policy is involved in many issues raised by public safety employees. An order to a police officer to remove a necklace was held not arbitrable on the grounds that arbitration would conflict with a strong public policy:

> There is involved here not only the safety of the police officer, but also the safety of the public since anything which poses a potential threat to the officer necessarily affects the quality of the protection afforded the public.[7]

## New York Experience

### Two-Tier Test for Arbitrability
October 18, 1977, the Court of Appeals of New York rendered its decision in the much-cited *Liverpool* case.[8] The court declared public sector labor arbitration to be "sufficiently different" from private sector labor arbitration on the basis

---

7. Incorporated Village of Malverne v. Malverne PBA, 72 A.D.2d 795, 421 N.Y.S.2d 624, 625 (1979).

8. Superintendent of Schools of Liverpool Central School District v. United Liverpool Faculty Ass'n, 42 N.Y.2d 509, 399 N.Y.S. 2d 189, 369 N.E.2d 746 (1977).

of the nondelegable responsibility of elected representatives in the public sector. The court prescribed a two-tier test for determining arbitrability of public sector cases. First, the court must determine whether the Taylor Law permits arbitration of a particular issue. Second, the court must determine whether the parties did in fact agree by the terms of the specific arbitration clause to arbitrate the particular issue.

*Liverpool* involved a female school teacher who, after an extended sick leave, was required to undergo a medical examination by a male doctor before returning to work. The teacher refused but indicated that she would participate in an examination by a female doctor. She was placed on a leave of absence without pay until the matter was resolved. She grieved the employer's action. The contract permitted arbitration of "claimed violation, misinterpretation or inequitable application of existing laws, rules, procedures, regulations, administrative orders or work rules of the District which relate to or involve teachers' health or safety, physical facilities, materials or equipment furnished to teachers or supervision of teachers." The contract also excluded arbitration of "any matter involving a teacher's rate of compensation, retirement benefit, or disciplinary proceeding." The court concluded that the issue could reasonably be held to be within both the included and excluded categories and that therefore it could not be said to be ". . . clearly and unequivocally within claims agreed to be referred to arbitration."[9]

The court held that in determining the scope of an arbitration clause,

> courts are to be guided by the principle that the agreement to arbitrate must be express, direct and unequivocal as to the is-

---

9. *Id.* at 515.

sues or dispute to be submitted to arbitration; anything less will lead to a denial of arbitration.[10]

The court rejected any presumption of arbitrability:

Indeed, inasmuch as the responsibilities of the elected representatives of the tax-paying public are overarching and fundamentally nondelegable, it must be taken, in the absence of clear unequivocal agreement to the contrary, that the board of education did not intend to refer differences which might arise to the arbitration forum. Such reference is not to be based on implication.[11]

*Arbitrability and the Law*

If a collective bargaining agreement conflicts with an imperative provision of law, the agreement is clearly void and unenforceable. Thus, a contract provision that denied transfer credits to employees who had been granted the credits by statute was held unenforceable.[12]

In *Syracuse Teachers Ass'n* v. *Board of Education,* the court declared that terms and conditions of employment are limited by "plain and clear" prohibitions in statutes or by case law.[13] An example of the court's application of this principle occurred in a case in which payment for out-of-title work was held to be inconsistent with the civil service procedures of testing and appointment of employees from civil service lists.[14] The reaction of public sector unions to this decision demonstrates a method sometimes available to public sector unions (in addition to their grievance procedures) to redress what they believe are inequitable situa-

---

10. *Id.* at 511.

11. *Id.* at 514.

12. Union Free School Dist. of Cheektowaga v. Nyquist, 38 N.Y.2d 137, 379 N.Y.S.2d 10, 341 N.E.2d 532 (1975).

13. 35 N.Y.2d 743, 361 N.Y.S.2d 912, 320 N.E.2d 646 (1974).

14. Burnell v. Anderson, N.Y.L.J. 11/26/75, p. 8, NYC Sp. Term pt. 1.

tions. Employee organizations lobbied the state legislature and obtained the enactment of the New York Civil Service Law §100,1(d) to permit such payments. A subsequent court case found arbitrable a grievance alleging out-of-title work. [15]

### Arbitrability and Public Policy

Arbitrability may also be limited by strong public policy: "Public policy whether derived from, and whether explicit or implicit in statute or decisional law, or in neither, may also restrict the freedom to arbitrate."[16] In a series of decisions, the court has narrowed its view of when contracts and public policy conflict. In *Board of Education of the City of New York* v. *Glaubman,* decided in 1981, the court issued an important decision qualifying its prior decision in *Liverpool:* "[W]e did not mean to suggest that hairsplitting analysis should be used to discourage or delay demands for arbitration in public sector contracts."[17] The court held that even though the education law contains substantive provisions regarding layoffs and recall, these were insufficient to force the conclusion that strong public policy precluded the parties from submitting to arbitration a dispute over their contractual recall provision. The court found the contract provision, which required rehiring on the basis of seniority, not to be in conflict with the statute, which addressed basic procedures but did not mandate a criterion for determining the order of recall.

In another case the court held that the scope of arbitration may be restricted by consideration of "objectively de-

15. County of Rockland v. Rockland County CSEA, 74 A.D.2d 812, 425 N.Y.S.2d 365 (1980).

16. Susquehanna Valley Central School Dist., *supra* note 1, at 616.

17. 53 N.Y.2d 781, 783, 439 N.Y.S.2d 907, 908, 422 N.E.2d 567, 568 (1981).

monstrable public policy."[18] Specifically, it ruled that the delegation of the statutory power to assign the grievant to a position as a permanent substitute did not preclude a contractual limitation on such assignment.

In *Port Jefferson Station Teachers* v. *Brookhaven-Comsewoque Union Free School District*, the court cautioned that only certain types of public policies are significant enough to justify voiding a collective bargaining provision.

> Incantations of "public policy" may not be advanced to overturn every arbitration award that impairs the flexibility of management of a school district. Every collective bargaining agreement involves some relinquishment of educational control by a school district. Only when the award contravenes a strong public policy, almost invariably involving an important constitutional or statutory duty or responsibility, may it be set aside.[19]

This case involved a contract provision that there would be no reduction in the number of specialist teachers as long as there was no decrease in enrollment. The court concluded that the employer school district

> certainly had the power to conclude that such services were necessary, and to agree to maintain them for the period of the collective bargaining agreement. No strong public policy however derived, is violated by such a provision in a short-term collective bargaining agreement.[20]

The following cases illustrate how the New York Court of Appeals has dealt with cases involving public policy. In a four-to-three decision, the court held that an arbitrator's award converting the discharge of an employee who admitted receiving unlawful gratuities to a six-month sus-

---

18. Board of Education of the Three Village Central Schools v. Three Village Teachers Ass'n, 82 A.D.2d 856, 440 N.Y.S.2d 47 (1981) (quoting Cheektowaga, *supra* note 12, at 143).

19. 45 N.Y.2d 898, 899, 411 N.Y.S.2d 1, 3, 383 N.E.2d 553, 554 (1978).

20. *Id.* at 900.

pension without pay should not be vacated as against public policy,[21] The majority of the court found that there was no public policy requiring that a bribe-receiving employee be discharged. Because three judges dissented, the dissent is worth noting:

> The basic tenor and direction of ethical standards governing conduct in municipal government should neither be molded by the pressures of collective bargaining nor left to the discretion of individual arbitrators.[22]

In another decision, a tie-in provision granting raises to administrators, which were based upon raises to teachers and were continued after expiration of the contract and during negotiations of a subsequent contract, was held not to violate public policy.[23] The court rejected the board of education's argument that the provision resulted in its loss of control over its ability to negotiate effectively and noted that nothing in the agreement assured that the teachers would get a raise in pay.

It is interesting to note the distinction between this case and *Viogt* v. *Bowen,* in which an appellate court found a wage parity clause unenforceable.[24] Although the parity provision was not expressly prohibited by statute, it was found to violate the statutory criteria used for resolving impasses for those parties subject to interest arbitration. The contract provision improperly limited wage comparisons to one specific group. The statute providing for interest arbitration did not cover boards of education, and that fact explains the difference in these two cases.

---

21. Binghamton Civil Service Forum v. City of Binghamton, 44 N.Y.2d 23, 403 N.Y.S.2d 482, 374 N.E.2d at 380.

22. *Id.* at 31.

23. Niagara Wheatfield Administrators Ass'n v. Niagara Wheatfield Central School Dist., 44 N.Y.2d 68, 404 N.Y.S.2d 82, 375 N.E.2d 37 (1978).

24. 53 A.D.2d 277, 385 N.Y.S.2d 600 (1976).

In *City of Oneida* v. *Oneida City Unit,* the fact that a position was exempt from civil service law did not signify to the court that the employer had a nondelegable right to fill the position, and it upheld an arbitration award in which the arbitrator found that the employer violated the contract provision dealing with the filling of vacancies and ordered appointment of the grievant with back pay.[25]

In *Burke* v. *Bowen,* the court determined that job security for a reasonable period of time is a permissive bargaining subject not inconsistent with any public policy so long as no financial emergency exists.[26] It considered the duration of the contract in question, three years and seven months, a reasonable period.

In another case, a subsequently declared financial emergency was held not to abrogate a job security provision because the financial emergency act provided that the employees' collective bargaining should not be impaired and specifically referred to attrition as the primary recourse to achieve a reduction in force.[27] The court pointed out a limitation on the parties' general powers, declaring that a collective bargaining agreement may not become a suicide pact, but it upheld the job security clause.

In bankruptcy all obligations may suffer impairment or dissolution, job security clauses included. But the collective bargaining agreement in question, negotiated before a legislatively declared emergency, short-term in length, and indistinguishable from the city's other contractual obligations which remain enforceable, is not yet vulnerable to attack as in violation of public policy.[28]

25. 78 A.D.2d 727, 432 N.Y.S. 2d 541 (1980).

26. 40 N.Y.2d 268, 386 N.Y.S.2d 657, 353 N.E.2d 569 (1976).

27. Board of Education v. Yonkers Federation of Teachers, 40 N.Y.2d 268, 386 N.Y.S.2d 657, 353 N.E.2d 569 (1976).

28. *Id.* at 276.

Job security guaranteed through indirection, such as a class size provision, has been held to be enforceable.[29] Class size, like job security, has been held to be a permissive collective bargaining subject.[30]

In a unique approach, the courts have distinguished between the right of the employer to commit itself and the right to commit its successors. One court has ruled that, when the sheriff is personally liable for the acts and omissions of his or her employees, a contract provision limiting removal of employees negotiated by the predecessor sheriff is not binding on the incumbent sheriff.[31] Such a provision or one limiting discipline is enforceable on the sheriff who negotiates it.[32]

A review of cases involving educational policy, and particularly the process leading to tenure, should point up the court's balancing of statutory and policy considerations against the right to bargain over terms and conditions of employment. The court held a violation of public policy occurred when a board of education contracted away its right to inspect personnel files.[33] Although the contract provision was not in direct conflict with education law, which imposed a duty to employ qualified teachers, grant tenure, and provide a written statement of reasons for denial of tenure upon request, it impaired the ability of the board to fulfill its statutory mandates. The law also made it a misdemeanor for the board to employ an unqualified teacher.

---

29. *Id.* at 386.

30. Susquehanna Valley Central School Dist., *supra* note 1.

31. Sirles v. Cordary, 49 A.D.2d 330, 374 N.Y.S.2d 793 (1975), *aff'd*, 40 N.Y.2d 950, 390 N.Y.S.2d 413, 358 N.E.2d 1038 (1976).

32. County of Broome v. Deputy Sheriffs Benevolent Ass'n, 57 A.D.2d 496, 395 N.Y.S. 2d 720 (1977).

33. Board of Education of Great Neck v. Areman, 41 N.Y.2d 527, 394 N.Y.S.2d 143, 362 N.E.2d 943 (1977).

While the board of education cannot bargain away its authority to make educational policy (such as to select curricular and educational material for students),[34] it can agree to submit a change in educational policy to an advisory board for its recommendations.[35]

The board of education has the discretion under the education law to grant or withhold tenure. While this power is nondelegable, it does not necessarily follow that all related powers are also nondelegable. A number of decisions have focused on the termination of a probationary employee and the concomitant tenure denial. The validity of a contract provision restricting the employer's substantive right to terminate a probationary employee is contingent upon whether the termination occurs during or at the end of the probationary period.[36] A clause restricting the unfettered right of the board to terminate a probationary employee at the end of the probation period is unenforceable as against public policy. But the power to terminate a probationary employee during the probationary period may be restricted by a contract provision. This distinction exists because continued employment of an employee at the end of the probationary period is usually tantamount to granting the employee tenure, and the tenure decision is nondelegable.

The board's power to determine whether to grant tenure does not relieve it of its obligation to adhere to contract procedures.[37] Thus, it has been held that the board's discretion to determine the method of evaluation may be lim-

---

34. Three Village Central Schools, *supra* note 18.

35. Wyandanch Union Free School Dist. v. Wyandanch Teachers Ass'n, 48 N.Y.2d 669, 421 N.Y.S. 2d 873, 397 N.E.2d 384 (1979).

36. Candor Central School Dist. v. Candor Teachers Ass'n, 42 N.Y.2d 266, 397 N.Y.S.2d 737, 366 N.E.2d 826 (1977).

37. Bellmore-Merrick Central High School Dist., *supra* note 4.

ited without encroachment upon its power to assess a teachers' performance.[38] The employer can commit itself either
to establish a contractual evaluation procedure[39] or to provide at least one written warning and a meeting of the employee, the supervisor, and a union representative for the
purpose of improving the employee's performance.[40] But if
the court determines that a claim that the grievant was improperly evaluated alleges no procedural deficiencies and is
attempting to challenge the evaluator's judgment, a stay of
the arbitration will be granted.

If a procedural violation is established, the arbitrator
has the authority to order temporary reinstatement without
tenure.

> The arbitrator's award did not abrogate the uncontroverted
> power of the board to determine, according to substantive cri-
> teria, which employees should be granted tenure. . . . Of
> course the arbitrator's award could not result in an automatic
> grant of tenure, thus rendering nugatory respondent's power to
> discharge a nontenured teacher.[41]

In regard to employees who have already been granted tenure, it has been held that, even though the statute deals
with discipline of tenured teachers, a board of education has
the power to enter into a contract providing that disciplinary action taken against tenured teachers is subject to
arbitration.[42]

---

38. Port Washington, *supra* note 6; Board of Education of Clarkstown School
Dist. v. Jones, 67 A.D.2d 537, 416 N.Y.S.2d 46 (1979).

39. Board of Education of Middle Island v. Middle Island Teachers Ass'n, 50
N.Y.2d 426, 429 N.Y.S.2d 564, 407 N.E.2d 411 (1980).

40. Candor Central Schol Dist., *supra* note 36.

41. Bellmore-Merrick Central High School Dist., *supra* note 4.

42. Associated Teachers of Huntington, *supra* note 1.

## Massachusetts Experience

Without explicitly applying a two-tier test of arbitrability, the Massachusetts Supreme Judicial Court deals with the two criteria raised in the *Liverpool* case in a similar manner as the New York Court of Appeals.

### Arbitrability and the Law

The determination of whether a contract conflicts with a statute and, if so, of which prevails is to some extent simplified by Massachusetts General Laws ch. 150E §7. This section delineates all the statutes that will be superseded by a conflicting contract provision. All other statutes prevail over an inconsistent contract provision.

In *Labor Relations Commission* v. *Town of Natick,* the court determined that a statute creating a strong police chief is subservient to a collective bargaining agreement; even though a police chief has authority over a bargaining subject, the selectmen may bargain over the subject, and the resultant contract will be enforceable against the police chief.[43] The decision relied on the fact that the statute creating a strong police chief was specifically listed in the state's collective bargaining law as being superseded by an inconsistent contract provision.

In *School Committee of Holyoke* v. *Duprey,* a contract provision requiring the employer to pay 65 percent of the employees' health insurance premiums was declared unenforceable because Massachusetts General Laws ch. 32B §7 limited the employer's contribution to 50 percent, and ch. 150E §7 did not specifically list that statute as being superseded by a contract provision.[44]

---

43. 369 Mass. 431, 339 N.E.2d 900 (1976).

44. School Committee of Holyoke, *supra* note 3.

When a particular statute is not listed in ch. 150E §7, the court must determine whether a matter is explicitly covered by the statute, implicitly covered by the statute, or, as a matter of public policy, is precluded from coverage in a collective bargaining agreement. If the court finds any of these situations, the matter will be held nonbargainable and, therefore, nonarbitrable. In order to determine the magnitude of public policy involved, a balancing test is applied by the court, as it did in *School Committee of Boston* v. *Boston Teachers' Union,* where its decision turned on

> whether the ingredient of educational policy in the issue subject to dispute is so comparatively heavy that collective bargaining, and even voluntary arbitration, on the subject is, as a matter of law, to be denied effect.[45]

In this case, the court affirmed an arbitrator's direction to the school committee that, pursuant to its contract, it consult with the union before instituting a policy change. The court noted that the arbitration award did not prevent eventual institution of the policy.

The court specifically declined to comment on whether, if a commissioner has the power (under a statute not listed in ch. 150E §7) to appoint and remove employees, that power could be abridged by a provision of a collective bargaining agreement.[46] Because job security is such a critical issue in collective bargaining, any future decision dealing with the specific issue of this case will have a significant effect on the parties involved. It seems clear that the legislature did not intend to preclude these employees from the right to bargain for a just cause provision and the inadvertent omission of that statute from the list points out a pitfall in attempting to list every relevant statute.

---

45. 378 Mass. 65, 389 N.E.2d 970 (1970).

46. Dwyer v. Commissioner of Insurance, 375 Mass. 227, 376 N.E.2d 826 (1978).

A recent decision aids greatly in resolving apparent conflicts between ch. 150E §7 and collective bargaining agreements. The court held that a statute containing a general grant of authority not embodying aspects of public policy, even though not listed in the section, does not transform otherwise mandatory collective bargaining subjects into nonmandatory subjects.[47]

## Arbitrability and Public Policy

A statute's description of a ministerial act will not be the basis for the finding of a policymaking function.[48]

An interesting distinction in the application of public policy is drawn by *City of Boston* v. *Boston Police Patrolmen's Association*[49] and *Mayor of Somerville* v. *Caliguri*.[50] In *Boston Police Patrolmen's Association*, a police officer was denied the return of his service revolver because he had not been psychiatrically evaluated as requested. The denial of the weapon resulted in deprivation of overtime and paid detail work. The arbitrator's award requiring the return of the service revolver was vacated because the head of the law enforcement department had the nondelegable authority to determine who shall carry a firearm. The *Mayor of Somerville* case involved a departmental decision to deny an officer a service revolver. He was then assigned to foot patrol in an area of town where he had previously been met with hostility. The arbitrator ordered that the officer be paid for the time he refused to patrol without a gun, but did not require

---

47. School Committee of Newton v. Labor Relations Commission, 388 Mass. 557 (1983).

48. Labor Relations Commission v. Selectmen of Dracut, 374 Mass. 619, 373 N.E.2d 1165 (1978).

49. 8 Mass. App. Ct. 220, 392 N.E.2d 1202 (1979).

50. 8 Mass. App. Ct. 335, 393 N.E.2d 958 (1979).

that the gun be returned to him. The court viewed the police chief's act more as an "imposition of a sentence rather than an exercise of his managerial powers. . . ."[51] and held this claim of statutory authority was nothing more than a pretense for effectuating personal hostility. This case is important because it establishes that, although the topic involved may be a nondelegable managerial right, it is nevertheless possible for an employer to abuse its discretion when allegedly exercising that right.

In *School Committee of Danvers* v. *Tyman,* the Supreme Judicial Court, noting its consistency with the New York decisions, held that enforcement of procedural safeguards in a contract did not interfere with the school committee's ultimate authority to grant or withhold tenure.[52] Citing *Warrior & Gulf,* the court announced a substantial burden on any party asserting nonarbitrability:

> Unless there is positive assurance that an arbitration clause is not susceptible to an interpretation that covers the asserted dispute, or unless no lawful relief conceivably can be awarded by the arbitrator an order to arbitrate should not be denied.[53]

In a case involving a job security clause, the Supreme Judicial Court held that in the context of public education, the clause was unenforceable for any period exceeding one year.[54] It is still unclear what effect this decision will have on the duration of public education labor contracts; the extent to which this decision will be applicable to noneducational public workers; or subjects related to the number of

---

51. *Id.* at 339.

52. 372 Mass. 106, 360 N.E.2d 877 (1977).

53. *Id.* at 113 (citing United Steelworkers of America v. Warrior & Gulf Navigation Co., 363 U.S. 574, 46 L.R.R.M. 2416 (1960)).

54. Boston Teachers Union, Local 66 v. School Committee of Boston, 386 Mass. 197, 434 N.E.2d 1258 (1982).

teachers employed (an issue in an earlier decision[55] cited in *Boston Teachers Union* in which the court had held clauses dealing with class size and teachers' load enforceable to the extent that there has been no change in educational policy or funding).

The Massachusetts decisions balancing educational policy and collective bargaining rights are basically similar to the New York decisions.

The remedy of back pay was determined to be valid for the failure to reappoint a grievant, but the remedy of reinstatement was held invalid because it conflicted with the statutory discretion of the superintendent of schools to make appointments.[56] In addition, the arbitrator could not order the school committee to appoint the grievant to the next position to become vacant.[57]

The abolition of a position has been held to also be a nondelegable decision.[58] While the authority to partially abolish a position is also nondelegable, if the decision is grieved, the arbitrator would have jurisdiction to hear a claim over the concomitant salary reduction.[59]

Despite the general rule that a school committee has the exclusive and nondelegable power to make appoint-

55. Boston Teachers Union v. School Committee of Boston, 370 Mass. 455, 350 N.E.2d 707 (1976).

56. Doherty v. School Committee of Boston, 363 Mass. 885, 297 N.E.2d 494 (1973).

57. School Committee of New Bedford v. New Bedford Educators Ass'n, 9 Mass. App. Ct. 793, 405 N.E.2d 162 (1980).

58. School Committee of Hanover v. Curry, 369 Mass. 683, 343 N.E.2d 144 (1976); School Committee of Braintree v. Raymond, 369 Mass. 686, 343 N.E.2d 145 (1976).

59. Lynnfield School Committee v. Trachtman, 1981 Mass. App. Ct. Adv. Sh. 541, 417 N.E.2d 459, *aff'd,* 1981 Mass. Adv. Sh. 2399.

ments of academic personnel,[60] the Supreme Judicial Court overruled the appeals court in *Blue Hills Regional District School Committee* v. *Flight.* In *Blue Hills,* an arbitrator granted a permanent appointment to a grievant claiming the school committee had abused its discretion by sexual discrimination. The appeals court vacated the arbitrator's award because the appointment power was nondelegable, but was overruled when the Supreme Judicial Court upheld the arbitrator's award and established an exception to the nondelegability doctrine. Citing New York authority, the court determined that an arbitrator may grant tenure if its denial was "for constitutionally impermissible reasons or in violation of statutory proscriptions."[61]

---

60. Berkshire Hills Regular School Dist. v. Berkshire Hills Education Ass'n, 375 Mass. 522, 377 N.E.2d 940 (1978).

61. Mass. Adv. Sh. (1981) 1240, 421 N.E.2d 755 (citing Cohoes City School Dist. v.Cohoes Teachers Ass'n, 40 N.Y.2d 774, 777, 390 N.Y.S.2d 53, 55, 358 N.E.2d 878, 880 (1976)).

# 10.

## The Scope of Public Sector Agreements

THE DEFINITION of a grievance is irrelevant if the subject matter sought to be arbitrated may not be delegated to the arbitrator for decision. Thus, a grievance covering the appointment of a principal was held nonarbitrable because the alleged violation did not relate to procedures but was substantive.[1] The contract clause, which provided preference for applicants already in the employ of the school district, was held unenforceable despite the agreement to arbitrate disputes over the interpretation of a contract provision.

### Grievance Definition

The courts have apparently found few, if any, collective bargaining agreements in the public sector in which a grievance is defined as "any dispute" between the parties. The cases usually concern contracts in which the grievance is defined as a violation, misinterpretation, or misapplication of

---

1. Berkshire Hills Regular School Dist. v. Berkshire Hills Education Ass'n, 375 Mass. 522, 377 N.E.2d 940 (1978).

the collective bargaining agreement. Sometimes this definition incorporates exclusionary language; one commonly cited exclusion restricts the grievance from covering "any matter for which a method of review is prescribed by law." The courts usually refer to these grievance definitions as "broad," and "narrow," respectively.[2]

## New York Experience

### No Excluded Matters
In applying its two-tier test of arbitrability, the New York courts make a major distinction between those grievance definitions that contain excluded areas and those that do not.

In a situation where the parties agree to arbitrate allegations of contract violations and misapplications without exception, the court determines arbitrability in a manner similar to that for a private sector grievance. So long as the agreement to arbitrate is unambiguous, the clarity of the substantive provision is irrelevant to arbitrability.

> The question of the scope of the substantive provisions of the contract is itself a matter of contract interpretation and application, and hence it must be deemed a matter for resolution by the arbitrator.[3]

The court has also held

> that the substantive provisions of the contract which are the subject of the grievance may be ambiguous does not serve to bar arbitration. It is a function of the arbitrator, and not the

---

2. South Colonie Central School Dist. v. South Colonie Teachers Ass'n, 46 N.Y.2d 521, 415 N.Y.S.2d 403, 388 N.E.2d 727 (1979).

3. Board of Education of Lakeland v. Barni, 49 N.Y.2d 311, 314, 425 N.Y.S.2d 554, 555, 401 N.E.2d 912, 913 (1980).

court to resolve any uncertainty as to those substantive rights and obligations of the parties.[4]

Also as in private sector cases, the court will not consider whether a claim is tenable or otherwise pass upon its merits.[5]

An appellate court decision analyzes the court's role.

In deciding whether a grievance is subject to arbitration, the courts are limited to determining whether there is a reasonable relationship between the subject matter of the dispute and the general subject matter of the underlying contract. . . . Penetrating definitive analysis of the scope of the agreement must be left to the arbitrators whenever the parties have broadly agreed that any dispute involving the interpretation and meaning of the agreement should be submitted to arbitration.[6]

In the following three cases, the court considered the issue one of contract interpretation and therefore arbitrable. In *South Colonie School District* v. *Longo,* a contract provision provided for no reprisals against "anyone" after a strike. The case was found arbitrable because the contract clause was susceptible to an interpretation that it covered a nonunit provisional employee.[7] The employer had challenged arbitrability on the basis that the grievance machinery is not applicable to an employee who is not a member of the bargaining unit. In *Board of Education of Roosevelt School District* v. *Roosevelt Teachers Association,* the court held arbitrable a claim that the contract clause delineating the salaries of sub-

---

4. Wyandanch Union Free School Dist. v. Wyandanch Teachers Ass'n, 48 N.Y.2d 669, 421 N.Y.S. 2d 873, 397 N.E.2d 384 (1979).

5. Board of Education, Bellmore-Merrick Central High School Dist. v. Bellmore-Merrick United Secondary Teachers, 39 N.Y.2d 167, 383 N.Y.S.2d 242, 347 N.E.2d 603 (1976).

6. County of Broome v. Deputy Sheriffs Benevolent Ass'n, 57 A.D.2d 496, 395 N.Y.S.2d 720 (1977).

7. 43 N.Y.2d 136, 400 N.Y.S.2d 798, 371 N.E.2d 516 (1977).

stitute teachers applied to per diem teachers.[8] In the third case, *Red Hook Central School District* v. *American Arbitration Association*, the school board established new positions to replace three positions that were in the bargaining unit but were abolished. The union's grievance was held arbitrable because an interpretation of the recognition clause was required.[9]

If the resolution of the arbitrability issue depends upon the finding of facts, the arbitrator is the one to determine the facts. Thus, it was the arbitrator who determined whether an individual was actually appointed to a job so as to obtain employee status.[10] But when the court determined that, as a matter of law, CETA employees were not employees of the school district against whom arbitration was sought, but of the town, a stay of arbitration was granted.[11]

### Excluded Matters

As a result of *Liverpool,* it is clear that when a dispute is arguably both included and excluded from the agreement to arbitrate, no presumption of arbitrability will be applied. In fact, one can conclude that in such a situation there is a presumption against arbitrability, because the burden on the party seeking to arbitrate is a substantial one.

> In such a case, it is impossible to conclude, as a court must conclude to direct that arbitration proceed, that the parties' agreement to arbitrate is "express, direct and unequivocal."[12]

---

8. 47 N.Y.2d 748, 417 N.Y.S.2d 252, 390 N.E.2d 1176 (1979).

9. 72 A.D.2d 816, 421 N.Y.S.2d 901 (1979).

10. Yonkers Federation of Teachers v. Board of Education of Yonkers, 60 A.D.2d 583, 399 N.Y.S.2d 891 (1977).

11. Dobbs Ferry School Dist. v. Dobbs Ferry United Teachers, 71 A.D.2d 673, 419 N.Y.S.2d 16 (1979).

12. South Colonie, *supra* note 2 at 526 (citing Superintendent of Schools of

In one case, the contract contained language relating to the arbitrator's authority but not specifically restricting any matter from arbitration. It warned that the arbitrator was prohibited from varying the terms of the contract or from usurping the discretionary functions of the employer. The court determined that the restrictive language was intended merely as a guide to the remedy once the arbitrator interpreted and applied the substantive provisions of the agreement. It was not considered a basis for granting a stay of the arbitration. In a footnote, the court pointed out that it was significant that the restrictive language was not expressly incorporated into the definition of a grievance. [13]

If the court can readily determine the inapplicability of exclusionary language to the specific grievance, it will refuse to grant a stay of the arbitration. In one case, the arbitration clause excluded matters for which the methods of review are prescribed by law. The grievance related to an assignment of the grievant to a position of permanent substitute. A hearing held under the education law established that the board was legally empowered to make such assignments. The court distinguished between the power to make the assignment and contractual limitation of that power. It concluded that the alleged contractual restriction had not been the subject of the statutory hearing and could be the subject of an arbitration hearing. [14]

Of course, if the grievance definition in the contract contains exclusionary language but the language is not re-

---

Liverpool Central School Dist. v. United Liverpool Faculty Ass'n, 42 N.Y.2d 509, 399 N.Y.S.2d 189, 369 N.E.2d 746 (1977)).

13. Lakeland, *supra* note 3; *id.* at n. 3.

14. Board of Education of Three Village Central Schools v. Three Village Teachers Ass'n, 82 A.D.2d 856, 440 N.Y.S.2d 47 (1981).

lied on by the party challenging arbitrability, the court will analyze the matter as if no exclusionary language exists.

## Massachusetts Experience

The Massachusetts courts have specifically declined to decide whether there is a presumption of arbitrability or of nonarbitrability in the public sector.[15]

The cases have not involved grievance definitions that contain exclusions. Where the definition is "an interpretation or application of the agreement," the Massachusetts courts, like the New York courts, have usually held that such interpretation and application is for the arbitrator and his or her decision on such matters is final and binding, subject only to the retention of nondelegable rights of the parties.[16]

The decision in *School Committee of Southbridge* v. *Brown,* which is inconsistent with the court's general approach of leaving contract interpretation questions to the arbitrator, appears to be an anomaly. That case involved a denial of a sabbatical leave, a matter the collective bargaining agreement put under the school committee's discretion. The court declared that the denial of a sabbatical leave was not an arbitrable issue, although a claim of inequitable or unfair application of the contract provision would be arbitrable.[17] The court appears to have gone beyond its role of interpreting the arbitration agreement and determining if the grievance comes within it. The court interpreted the sub-

---

15. School Committee of Southbridge v.Brown, 375 Mass. 502, 377 N.E.2d 935 (1978).

16. School Committee of Danvers v.Tyman, 372 Mass. 106, 360 N.E.2d 877 (1977); *see also* Dennis-Yarmouth Regional School Committee v. Dennis Teachers Ass'n, 372 Mass. 116, n. 4, 360 N.E.2d 883, n. 4 (1977).

17. Southbridge, *supra* note 15.

stantive provision of the contract so as to preclude any challenge to the discretion of the school committee. In *School Committee of Danvers* v. *Tyman*, the same court noted approvingly the *Warrior & Gulf* standard that unless there is positive assurance that the arbitration clause does not cover the dispute, it is arbitrable. By application of this standard, the grievance in Southbridge should have been held arbitrable.[18]

18. Danvers, *supra* note 16 (citing United Steelworkers of America v. Warrior & Gulf Navigation Co., 363 U.S. 574, 46 L.R.R.M. 2416 (1960)).

# 11.

## The Review of
## Public Sector Awards

### When the Arbitrability Issue Is Raised

A PARTY MAY challenge the validity of an arbitration award on the basis that the contract clause contravenes a statute, decisional law, or public policy and is therefore unenforceable. This issue may be raised by a party for the first time in appellate court after the arbitration award, or it may be raised by the court on its own motion.[1] This type of challenge to an arbitration award can be raised in court even though the employer voluntarily submitted the grievance to arbitration.[2]

Even when the parties submitted the arbitrability issue to the arbitrator, who found the matter to be arbitrable, the award may be vacated if the court determines the matter is not within the scope of the authorities of the parties.[3] Thus,

---

1. Niagara Wheatfield Administrators Ass'n v. Niagara Wheatfield Central School Dist., 44 N.Y.2d 68, 404 N.Y.S.2d 82, 375 N.E.2d 37 (1978).

2. School Committee of Hanover v. Curry, 369 Mass. 683, 343 N.E.2d 144 (1976).

3. Dennis-Yarmouth Regional School Committee v. Dennis Teachers Ass'n, 372 Mass. 116, 360 N.E.2d 883 (1977).

if an employer cannot bind itself, it cannot delegate to an arbitrator the authority to bind it.[4]

The New York courts have treated differently a claim that the issue arbitrated is beyond the scope of the arbitration agreement. In such a situation, the party challenging the arbitrator's award will be held to have waived its right to object by participating in the arbitration.[5] The New York courts find an inherent conflict when a party submits an issue to arbitration and later seeks to assert that the arbitrator had no power to resolve the issue.

Although the Massachusetts courts have not dealt directly with this issue, there is every reason to assume their decisions would be similar to that of the New York courts.

## Standard of Review

The statutory authority for vacating a grievance arbitration award delineates the grounds for such action. In New York, this is Civil Practice Laws and Rules §7511, in Massachusetts, General Laws ch. 150c §11. These standards should not be confused with those for reviewing interest arbitrations.

The court's review of the arbitrator's award does not extend to mistakes of law or fact unless fraud is involved.[6] (This of course does not cover an error of law as to the scope

---

4. School Committee of Holyoke v. Duprey, 8 Mass. App. Ct. 58, 391 N.E.2d 925 (1979) (citing Hanover, *supra* note 2, and Susquehanna Valley Central School Dist. v. Susquehanna Valley Teachers Ass'n, 37 N.Y.2d 614, 376 N.Y.S.2d 427, 339 N.E.2d 132 (1975)).

5. Binghamton Civil Service Forum v. City of Binghamton, 44 N.Y.2d 23, 403 N.Y.S.2d 482, 374 N.E.2d 380 (1978).

6. School Committee of West Springfield v. Korbut, 4 Mass. App. Ct. 743, 358 N.E.2d 831 (1976); Associated Teachers of Huntington v. Board of Education of Huntington, 33 N.Y.2d 229, 351 N.Y.S.2d 670, 306 N.E.2d 791 (1973).

of either party's authority, which may always be raised in court for the first time.) The court followed this approach when noting,

> The record presented to us provides no support for this fact, but we treat it as one proven because of our limited review of factual determinations in arbitration disputes.[7]

In *Rochester City School District* v. *Rochester Teachers Association,* the court noted its limited review and declared that the award would not be vacated unless the arbitrator was wholly irrational. It went on to say that the arbitrator may do justice by applying the spirit rather than the letter of the agreement.

> Thus courts may not set aside an award because they feel that the arbitrator's interpretation disregards the apparent, or even the plain, meaning of words or resulted from a misapplication of settled legal principles. In other words a court may not vacate an award because the arbitrator has exceeded the power the court would have, or would have had if the parties had chosen to litigate, rather than arbitrate the dispute. Those who have chosen arbitration as their forum should recognize that arbitration procedures and awards often differ from what may be expected in courts of law.[8]

A standard enunciated in *School Committee of Danvers* v. *Tyman* is

> Judicial intervention is not warranted where no conflict has arisen between the consequences of the arbitration proceedings called for in the collective bargaining agreement and any non-delegable authority of the school committee.[9]

In the *Danvers* case, the court found no conflict between the arbitrator's authority to enforce a procedural right and the committee's ultimate authority to determine whether or not

---

7. City of Boston v. Boston Police Patrolmen's Association, 8 Mass. App. Ct. 220, 392 N.E.2d 1202 (1979).

8. Rochester City School Dist. v. Rochester Teachers Ass'n, 41 N.Y.2d 578, 398 N.Y.S.2d 179, 362 N.E.2d 977 (1977); *id.* at 582.

9. School Committee of Danvers v. Tyman, 372 Mass. 106, 111, 360 N.E.2d 877, 881 (1977).

to grant tenure. In a companion case, the court approvingly cites the New York decision in the *Bellmore-Merrick* case, in which a temporary reinstatement to remedy a procedural violation was approved. [10]

When a teacher evaluation procedure was violated and the grievant's position was abolished, an order to compensate the grievant for all or part of the subsequent school year was held valid. [11]

To the extent the arbitrator's award is based upon his or her view of a statute's inherent public policy conflicting with the contract, a one-way appeal is set up. If the arbitrator holds that the contract was not violated or declines to order a meaningful remedy, the union would have no basis for judicial appeal. But if the arbitrator determines that a public policy does not exist, the public employer can obtain judicial review of the decision.

## Past Practice

If the grievance definition is limited to contract violations, past practice may not serve as a basis for the arbitrator's award. [12] But if the definition of grievance is sufficiently broad to encompass past practices, it may. Thus, a definition that included a claim affecting terms and conditions of employment was broad enough to include past practice. [13]

---

10. School Committee of West Bridgewater v. West Bridgewater Teachers Ass'n, 372 Mass. 121, 360 N.E.2d 886 (1977) (citing Board of Education, Bellmore-Merrick Central School Dist. v. Bellmore-Merrick United Secondary Teachers, 39 N.Y.2d 167, 383 N.Y.S.2d 242, 347 N.E.2d 603 (1976)).

11. *Id.*

12. Superintendent of Schools of Liverpool Central School Dist. v. United Liverpool Faculty Ass'n, 42 N.Y.2d 509, 399 N.Y.S.2d 189, 369 N.E.2d 746 (1977).

13. Essex County Board of Supervisors v. CSEA, 67 A.D.2d 1047, 413 N.Y.S.2d 722 (1979).

Past practice can always be used to assist in interpreting a substantive provision of the contract.[14] In addition, a substantive contract provision may establish a right to have past practices continued during the contract term. An example of this is a provision that employer policies that remain unaltered by the contract shall remain in effect.

A contract provision containing a salary schedule was held subject to the practice of giving credit for certain experience despite the fact that the contract contained a zipper clause. The zipper clause was held not to "prevent interpretation and application of the agreement in accordance with past practice."[15] The court noted its limited role by stating, "Once it is decided that a matter is arbitrable, we do not decide the merits."[16] Reference to past practice was considered to be a common source to assist in interpreting a contract provision, and therefore the court held that the award drew its essence from the contract.

## Remedy

The general rule is that the arbitrator has broad remedial discretion.[17] The issue of whether the arbitrator has exceeded his or her powers is subject to review.[18]

The limitation relating to the parties' authority is, of course, applicable in regard to remedy just as in regard to

---

14. Corinth Central School Dist. v. Corinth Teachers Ass'n, 77 A.D.2d 366, 434 N.Y.S.2d 725 (1980); Rochester City School Dist., *supra* note 8.

15. Chief Administrative Justice of the Trial Court v. SEIU Local 254, 1981 Mass. Adv. Sh. 1457, 422 N.E.2d 776 (1981).

16. *Id.* at 1460.

17. Triton Regional School Committee v. Triton Teachers Ass'n, 7 Mass. App. Ct. 873, 386 N.E.2d 767 (1979).

18. Holyoke, *supra* note 4.

arbitrability. Thus, when a municipality was legally barred from making payments to a union scholarship, an arbitrator's order to make such payments to remedy a school committee's violation of its agreement to hire substitute teachers was vacated.[19]

In another case, the arbitrator was aware that the school committee could not legally implement its contract commitment to pay more than 50 percent of employees' health insurance premiums. He, therefore, ordered the committee to pay monetary damages directly to the teachers. The monetary damages equaled the cost of that portion of the premium that the committee could not pay.[20] The award was vacated by the court because the arbitrator had no authority to award damages to the union for the school committee's decision not to violate the law.

---

19. Boston Teachers Union v. School Committee of Boston, 370 Mass. 455, 350 N.E.2d 707 (1976).

20. Holyoke, *supra* note 4.

# 12.

## A Summary Guide
## to the Issues

ARBITRABILITY IS the determination of the arbitrator's jurisdiction to hear the grievance on its merits. The *scope of the
arbitrator's authority,* as used in this book, refers to the authority of the arbitrator to make rulings during the hearing,
to issue awards, and to impose remedies as part of the
award.

It is in everyone's interest to have the jurisdiction and
authority of the arbitrator understood from the outset. To
go through the long grievance-arbitration procedure only to
have a final award blocked before its issuance or vacated afterward is an expense of time and money that could have
been more efficaciously used to find another means of resolving the underlying problem.

Union and management practitioners may, and often
do, agree to submit issues of arbitrability to the arbitrator.
It is important to have a clear understanding of which issues
the court will allow to be fully litigated before it and which
issues the court will presume to be arbitrable and will routinely pass along to be resolved by the arbitrator. It is also

important to know which decisions by the arbitrator may be challenged and on what basis.

## When and Where Issues May Be Raised

Challenges to the arbitrator's jurisdiction or scope of authority may be raised in court before the arbitration, during it, or after the issuance of an arbitration award. The challenges may be raised in an action to enjoin the arbitration, to vacate an arbitration award, or in defense of a motion by the successful party to confirm the award.

An important limitation is that, once a party participates in the arbitration hearing, he or she may not raise a claim that the grievance does not fall within the ambit of the parties' agreement to arbitrate.

Claims that an award contravenes public policy (usually a public sector issue) may always be raised in court, and the court may, on its own motion, raise the issue in a pending case dealing with the confirmation of the award.

Procedural arbitrability issues, questions of whether contractual procedure has been followed, have been routinely held to be for the arbitrator to resolve. These issues are viewed as questions of contract interpretation or application and as such are routinely held to be within the scope of the arbitration clause.

## Types of Issues

Four general types of issues are raised:

1. Is a party a proper party, one covered by an agreement to arbitrate?

2. Did a party agree to arbitation?

3. Does the grievance fall within the scope of the arbitration agreement?

4. Has the arbitrator's rulings or award exceeded his or her authority?

## Proper Party

A claim that a party is not bound by the collective bargaining agreement alleged to be violated is for the court to resolve. It could be said either that there is no presumption of arbitrability in this type of case or that any presumption is counterbalanced by other policy considerations. In cases in which the presumption of arbitrability is not applied, the court will review all available evidence and render a decision resolving the issue.

## Agreement to Arbitrate

The courts will not require arbitration in absence of an agreement to be bound by arbitration. If there is no agreement to arbitrate, the aggrieved party has the right to enforce its contract through the courts. If the issue in court is whether a party has entered into an agreement to arbitrate, there is no presumption of arbitrability.

To ascertain that an agreement to arbitrate covers a particular grievance, it must be determined that the agreement took effect and that the alleged violation either arose during the term of the agreement or constituted a right accrued during the term of the contract and intended to be realized after the expiration of the contract.

## Scope of the Arbitration Agreement

In the famous Steelworkers Trilogy cases, the United States Supreme Court determined that as a matter of federal policy, grievance arbitration is the desirable method for resolving private sector labor disputes. This applies to claims challenging whether the grievance comes within the scope of the arbitration agreement. In these cases, the burden on the party arguing nonarbitrability is extremely high. The court will find the matter arbitrable unless it can be shown with positive assurance that the matter is not arbitrable. The court will not consider whether a claim is tenable nor otherwise pass upon its merits.

The main factor in determining whether a claim falls within the ambit of the arbitration clause is the contract's definition of the term grievance. A broad definition specifies that "any dispute" may be raised in arbitration, and under it the aggrieved party is not limited to a claimed violation of the contract.

A more limited definition restricts the aggrieved party to claims that the contract was violated. In these cases, the court will not attempt to prejudge the matter by examining the contract language that is claimed to have been violated; it will determine only whether the language could be interpreted in a manner that would sustain the union's claim. The contract language may not even deal specifically with the matter sought to be arbitrated.

A third type of case is one in which the contract provides that certain matters are to be excluded from arbitration. The private sector policy favoring arbitration applies, and consequently there is an extremely high burden on the party challenging arbitrability.

If a dispute is apparently covered both by a contract provision not subject to arbitration and one that is subject to arbitration, the court will determine which clause governs on the basis of which is more specific.

If there is no dispute over the meaning of the exclusionary language, but there is a factual disagreement over whether a particular situation falls within the exclusionary language, the arbitrator is to resolve the dispute.

If a broad action by management is not reviewable in arbitration, a challenge to such action is generally not arbitrable. If, however, an action based on a particular reason or motivation is excluded from arbitration, it is for the arbitrator to determine the motivating factor in a specific case.

## Public Sector

The main differences between public and private sector arbitrability questions are in the areas of authority of the parties and presumption of arbitrability. While the general rule that the arbitrator can have no greater authority than the parties is applicable to both sectors, the rule is rarely relevant in the private sector but is frequently raised in the public sector.

In determining whether a claim is arbitrable, the public sector cases deal with an issue that is almost nonexistent in the private sector. That question is whether the law authorizes arbitration with respect to the particular issue. In answering this question, a presumption of arbitrability is not applied. The contractual definition of the term grievance is irrelevant, because the subject matter sought to be arbitrated may not be delegated to the arbitrator for decision. The court balances the labor relations interests with other interests to ascertain whether a subject is or is not a prohibited bargaining subject. If a subject sought to be arbitrated is a prohibited bargaining subject, the parties do not have the requisite authority to effectuate an agreement over the subject. Therefore, an arbitrator may not interpret the contract to effect the prohibited bargaining subject. For example, the decision to grant tenure in a school district has been held to be a nondelegable managerial right and, thus, a prohibited bargaining subject; the managerial right should not be confused with the procedures that lead to the final determination, a mandatory bargaining subject, which can be the subject of an arbitration.

The follow principles may help in determining whether the parties do or do not have authority to make a commitment in a particular area:

1. Statutes, decisional law, or public policy may be the basis for finding a claim beyond the scope of the parties' authority.

2. While in other contexts there is a significant distinction between permissive and mandatory collective bargaining subjects, in issues of arbitrability, the distinction is immaterial. So long as the parties have the authority to commit themselves on the subject, the arbitrator may properly enforce an agreement he or she determines the parties have made.

3. The particular remedy requested does not have any relevance to whether the claim is arbitrable. The remedy requested is merely a suggestion and does not limit the arbitrator's authority. When there is no permissible remedy, the grievance will be held nonarbitrable.

4. Most subjects are not entirely either prohibited bargaining subjects or permissible bargaining subjects. Should the court not be able to determine the precise nature of the grievance, it will permit arbitration subject to review of the award.

The courts balance the labor relations interests with other interests to ascertain whether a subject is or is not a prohibited bargaining subject. A presumption of arbitrability is not applied. In determining whether a particular subject is prohibited, the New York and Massachusetts courts have arrived at some interesting compromises in their efforts to balance the competing interests.

In determining whether a grievance is within the scope of the parties' arbitration agreement, the courts generally apply the same policy favoring arbitrability that is applied in the private sector cases. In New York, a negative presumption has been determined if the claim is arguably covered by both inclusionary and exclusionary language of the grievance clause.

While a claim that a grievance is not within the scope of the arbitration agreement must be raised before the issuance of the award, a claim that a subject matter is beyond the scope of the parties' authority may be raised for the first time during judicial appeal.

A final caveat on public sector arbitrability: each state has its own collective bargaining law, other potentially conflicting statutes, and public policy. The interplay of these must be examined to determine how specific claims would be treated in any particular state.

## Arbitrator's Award and Judicial Review

The arbitrator is permitted wide latitude in fashioning a remedy. The following are limitations on the arbitrator's power:

1. The remedy must be limited to the specific issue submitted to the arbitrator.

2. The arbitrator may not order a party to commit an unfair labor practice or an illegal act.

3. The arbitrator has no authority to award punitive damages.

4. An arbitrator cannot order the parties to do anything which they do not otherwise have authority to do.

In general, an award will be vacated only if it was procured by fraud, the arbitrator's partiality is established, or the arbitrator exceeds his or her authority. A mistake of law or fact is not sufficient basis for vacating an arbitration award. In this aspect, an award is more binding than a decision of a court of initial jurisdiction. Unless the award compels the violation of law or conduct contrary to strong public policy, an error of law is not a basis for reversal. Of course, if an arbitrator renders an award that conflicts with a nondelegable managerial right, the award can be vacated as a violation of public policy, whether that policy is stated in a statute or based upon court decision. While this type of issue is almost nonexistent in the private sector, it frequently arises in the public sector.

The award will be confirmed if it can in any rational way be derived from the agreement and reversed only if there is a manifest disregard for the principles of contract interpretation and the common law of the shop. The court relies heavily on the arbitrator's judgment in interpreting contract language, identifying the common law, finding fact and finding of law.

The general principle in regard to most issues of the arbitrator's authority is that the court does apply a presumption favoring the legality of the award. Doubts are resolved in favor of enforcement.

In determining whether an award conflicts with a prohibited bargaining subject, such as a nondelegable right, the court does not apply a presumption in favor of legality. The court permits a limited review of the manner in which the nondelegable managerial right was exercised. If the statutory authority is nothing more than a pretext for effectuating personal hostility, an award of monetary damages will be upheld. Although the topic involved may be a nondelegable managerial right, it is nevertheless possible for an employer to abuse its discretion when exercising that right.

The authority of the arbitrator is determined by the powers conveyed to him or her by the parties through the contract's arbitration clause. (This authority is, of course, limited by the authority the parties actually possess.) The importance of a stipulated issue jointly submitted to the arbitrator cannot be overstated. When the parties submit an agreed upon issue to the arbitrator, they are making a specific agreement, limited in its application to that case. But the stipulated issue may have the effect of expanding or reducing the authority that the arbitrator would otherwise have.

The award also must draw its essence from the contract. Even though a claim may have been held to be arbitrable before the hearing, the ensuing arbitration award may be vacated if it is rendered without a proper basis.

The court will uphold the award if any proper basis exists, even if that basis is not mentioned in the arbitration award. The arbitrator is not required to explain the basis of his or her award. The courts, however, encourage the arbitrator to explain the reasoning. But if the arbitrator's explanation discloses an improper basis for the award, it will be vacated.

The court will not enforce an award that is incomplete, ambiguous, or contradictory. It will not clarify an ambiguous award, but will remand it to the arbitrator for clarification.

## Role of the Parties

Subject to their legal powers, the employer and the union establish the jurisdiction and scope of authority of the arbitrator by defining a grievance in their collective bargaining agreement and, where applicable, by amending that definition by their submission of the issue to the arbitrator. Should the parties have a disagreement over the arbitrator's jurisdiction or scope of authority, the court is the final determiner.

If practitioners acquire a better understanding of the issues relating to arbitrability and the scope of the arbitrator's authority, pointless and unnecessary litigation will be avoided and the parties' labor relations will be greatly enhanced.

# Index to Cases Cited

# General Index